Research Methods in Health, Care and Early Years

Karen Hucker

Heinemann Educational Publishers,
Halley Court, Jordan Hill, Oxford OX2 8EJ
A division of Reed Educational & Professional Publishing Ltd

Heinemann is a registered trademark of Reed Educational & Professional Publishing Limited

OXFORD MELBOURNE AUCKLAND JOHANNESBURG BLANTYRE GABORONE IBADAN PORTSMOUTH NH (USA) CHICAGO

© Karen Hucker 2001

First published 2001
2005 2004 2003 2002 2001
10 9 8 7 6 5 4 3 2 1

A catalogue record for this book is available from the British Library on request.

ISBN 0 435 40168 8

Pages designed by Wendi Watson

Typeset and illustrated by Saxon Graphics Ltd, Derby

Printed and bound in Great Britain by Scotprint, East Lothian
Tel: 01865 888058 www.heinemann.co.uk

Acknowledgements

I would like to thank Martin for his continued support and encouragement. I would also like to thank Linda Johnson for taking the time to read the text and give valuable advice, encouragement and ideas. I have also appreciated the support and guidance from Mary and Anna at Heinemann, which has helped ensure the book reached completion.
Karen Hucker

The authors and publisher would like to thank the following individuals and organisations for permission to reproduce photographs and other copyright material.

page 8 (left) – Rupert Horrocks; page 8 (right) – Liz Eddison; pages 23, 66 – Crown Copyright material is reproduced under Class License Number C01W004 with the permission of the Controller of HMSO and the Queen's Printer for Scotland; pages 51 (top left, bottom left), 149 (top right) – Department of Health publications – further copies are available from Department of Health, PO Box 777, London SE1 6XH; page 51 (top right) – Crown copyright material is reproduced with the permission of the Controller of Her Majesty's Stationery Office; page 51 (bottom right) – Reproduced with permission from the Royal College of Nursing; pages 55, 56 – Google.com; page 62 – Birth Certificate © Crown copyright – Office for National Statistics. Reproduced with the permission of the Controller of HMSO; page 77 – 'One nurse in three "is ready to resign"' by Paul Kendall from the *Daily Mail* on 7 May 2001 – article reproduced with permission of the *Daily Mail*; page 78 (left) – 'Byers to promise leave for adoptive parents' by Nigel Morris from *The Independent* on 7 May 2001 – article reproduced with permission of *The Independent*; page 78 (right) – 'Shopping maul. Stores losing out as we find new ways to spend our cash' by Clinton Manning from *The Mirror* on 8 May 2001 – article reproduced with permission of the *The Mirror*; page 86 – 'Middle-class children more prone to allergies' by David Derbyshire from *The Daily Telegraph* on 5 July 2000 – article reproduced with permission of *The Daily Telegraph*; pages 131, 137 – Gareth Boden; page 149 (top left and bottom right) – SMA Nutrition; page 149 (bottom left) – H. J. Heinz Company Limited.

Every effort has been made to contact copyright holders of material published in this book. We would be glad to hear from unacknowledged sources at the first opportunity.

Dedication

For Martin, Abigail and George

Contents

Introduction

Most courses allow students opportunities to develop research skills. In many subjects, students have to complete a research project of some kind in order to achieve their final qualification. Some of these will be bigger pieces of work than others.

This book aims to explain the research process and outline the different methods of research clearly. It is set out in such a way that you can read the whole text or dip into the chapters that are relevant to you – each chapter stands on its own. Therefore, if you are using a questionnaire, the chapter on questionnaires gives you all you need to know.

The book also helps you to plan the whole process of research – from choosing your idea to writing up the final piece of work. It takes you through the process of focusing your work into an achievable research project and helps you plan out what you are going to do.

The main focus of the book is on how to carry out the various research methods that you may choose to use. Each chapter explains how to carry out one particular method and how to avoid any problems that might arise. The chapters also give you tips on how to ensure your research is valid and reliable.

Checklists are scattered throughout the book to help you make sure that you haven't missed out any part of the process. There is also a terminology list in Chapter 1 to ensure you understand the words that are commonly used in research.

At the end of each chapter there is an activity to check you have understood the contents of that chapter. Trying these out will help ensure you complete the research process accurately.

PART **1**

Types of research methods

I The basics of research

A good research project or investigation is dependent on the way the research is carried out. This book is all about how to carry out research effectively. It explains the different methods of research and helps to point out where mistakes can be easily made. Following these guidelines will help you to carry out effective research which will be relevant to the focus of your work.

This first chapter sets research in context. It explains why research is important and what it actually is. It also covers the different types of research which will help you in the area of health, care and early years. The chapter also looks at issues which influence the way research is carried out, such as ethics and human rights.

This chapter covers:

◆ What is research?

◆ Why do you need to know about research?

◆ Research terminology

◆ Types of research

◆ Types of research methods

◆ Quantitative and qualitative methods of research

◆ Triangulation

◆ Ethics in research

◆ Applying ethics in the research process

◆ Data Protection Act 1998.

What is research?

Research is the way in which we find out new things. In all types of work, people use different methods of research to find out new information or to analyse how they might do something better or more efficiently.

Research is an organised activity which is carried out in a systematic manner in order to find out information and gain knowledge. It can range from scientific experiments which are trying to find a cure for an illness, to a local health centre carrying out a questionnaire survey with its patients to see how its service might be improved.

Carrying out a questionnaire survey into people's shopping habits

There are lots of assumptions made about what happens in society. This means that people draw conclusions about issues which they may not have any 'evidence' for. You may have heard statements about girls doing better than boys at school or that children aren't as fit as they used to be. In conversation, people make such statements as if they are 'common knowledge'; whereas the purpose of research is to provide evidence to support statements that are made. The research may prove or disprove the statements. The results of research can make people change their minds about something, or help them to decide what action to take to improve or change something.

Research is carried out by lots of different groups of people for many different reasons. This includes companies, manufacturers, local and central government, service providers such as the health service, voluntary organisations and individuals.

Make a list of three different groups of people that you can think of who may carry out research in health and social care.

Identify a reason why they might carry out research.

Why do you need to know about research?

In most advanced courses, students are encouraged to develop research skills. This may be used for a small piece of coursework such as an observation on a child relating to a particular aspect of development, or a questionnaire on an issue linked to the specifications. Some subjects also require you to carry out a detailed investigation or research project as part of the assessment. In this case, you are likely to use more than one research method to do this piece of work.

How can this book help you?

The book can guide you through the planning process and help you choose an appropriate topic to study. It will help you think through your ideas and ensure you have a topic which you can realistically investigate given your time and resources. It will give you pointers to help you stay on track with the work.

This book identifies the different research methods you could use and explains how they should be carried out. It gives the strengths and weaknesses of each method so you can make an informed choice about which ones suit your topic and approach best. The book can be read cover to cover, but it is more likely that once you have decided what you are doing, and the methods you wish to use, that you dip into the appropriate chapters in more depth.

There is also a number of checklists to use which will show if you have missed out key parts of any method or of the project itself.

Research terminology

There are a number of specific terms associated with research. This means that it uses certain words that mean something particular in the research process. The list below explains some of the words you may come across when you are carrying out your research.

Terms associated with research

Confidentiality. Being confidential means that you will not repeat what someone else has told you to others. In research, this means not giving any real names. Usually codes or false names are used. This helps ensure that information cannot be traced back to any one individual – important if you want people to be open and frank with you. Many forms of research, especially primary research methods, rely on people giving you personal information about themselves, their thoughts and beliefs. Being confidential is important for good research.

Data. This covers facts, statistics and perceptions. Results from different research methods are known as data. Data has to be interpreted; data which has not been interpreted is known as raw data.

Data Protection Act. This Act gives people the right to look at any information which is kept on file about them. It also gives guidelines on what information can be collected and how long it can be kept.

Methodology. This is the study of the research techniques that may be used. Methodology looks at how you carry out your chosen method in terms of who you choose to ask (your sample) and how you ensure you get a good response rate. It includes how you ensure that the method produces reliable and valid data. There is more information on reliability and validity in Chapter 4.

Objective. Being objective is an important part of research. This means that you are able to look at the information you have and analyse it without bias or introducing any pre-conceived ideas you may hold. This means you report what you find and do not add any points that cannot be proven through the research. It is not easy to be fully objective as it is part of human nature to hold opinions, which can influence the conclusions we draw from our research findings. However, being aware of this can help researchers to be as objective as possible.

Primary research. This is research that you carry out personally and therefore the findings are original to the person conducting the research. This doesn't mean that you are looking at an area that no one has ever looked at before, but the information is collected by you and therefore is new to you. Information collected by others but not analysed is considered raw data. Therefore, it is regarded as primary research.

Primary research methods. These are research methods used by the researchers themselves to gather first-hand information from people. The methods include interviews, questionnaires and observations.

Qualitative. This covers the type of research which aims to get personal views and opinions from people. It aims to look at things in depth and therefore is more concerned with the quality of the responses given rather than the quantity. It is less about how much, and more about what and why. Research methods which are classed as qualitative include interviews and observations. This is because these types of research method produce a lot of detailed information which is not in a statistical format.

Quantitative. This covers research methods which aim to look at how many people think something. It is concerned with numbers and statistics. The research methods are designed to collect a lot of data which can then be analysed and catagorised in order to draw conclusions and make sense of the findings. Research methods which are classed as quantitative include questionnaires.

Raw data. Data which has not been interpreted or analysed.

Reliability. This means that your method produces information which could be replicated.

Research ethics. Ethics are about carrying out your research in a morally correct way, and considering how your research methods may affect the people involved and if the methods are acceptable. For example, you cannot force people to give you information, or collect and hold data which is not relevant to your research. This also includes the issue of seeking permission when carrying out research on individuals, especially children.

Research methods. These are the techniques you are going to use to investigate the topic, such as questionnaires, interviews, observations, etc.

Sampling. This is the way you select who you are going to involve in your research. For example, how you decide who you are going to give your questionnaires to. There are many different sampling methods; which one you use depends on what you are researching and the potential number of people who could be involved.

Secondary research. This is using information that has already been produced by other people. It includes information in books or newspapers. It can also include findings of other people's research. The key point is that it isn't original work that you have carried out.

Secondary research methods. These draw on previously published work and would include research using textbooks, the Internet and magazines.

Subjective. Being subjective means bringing your own thoughts and emotions to an issue, and not basing your comments only on the information that has been found. Work based purely on your own personal views is not valuable research as it does not really inform us of what is actually happening. It does not score highly in assessed work.

Survey. This is an umbrella term for questionnaires, interviews and data collection surveys.

Validity. This means that your research method produces information which is relevant to the topic you are looking at.

Types of research

There are a number of different types of research. Some of these are set out below with examples of how they might be used.

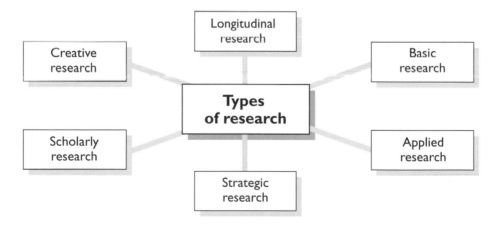

Basic research

This type of research is based around finding out about an issue or subject with no particular reason other than the wish to investigate it. There is no intention to use the findings in any particular way.

EXAMPLE

Research into a woman's role in the family. The research would look at the theory and then carry out some investigatory work to see if the theories are reflected in the findings. Conclusions would then be drawn regarding the similarities and differences found between the results and the theories. However, this work would not be used to change the role of women in the family. That would be impossible to do.

Applied research

This type of research is based around the wish to find out something specific. The findings can usually be used in some practical way.

EXAMPLE

Research into how fitness might be improved with certain exercise regimes or research into management practices in care homes. In both these cases, the findings from the research could be applied to a real situation with the aim of improving what is happening.

Strategic research

This aspect of research applies to work in areas which are new and emerging. It may be that the subject is not yet developed enough for anyone to know what the practical applications might be. However, it is the way in which society advances its thinking, knowledge and skills. Often funding for this type of research comes from the government.

EXAMPLE

This type of research might be used to develop equipment out of new materials to improve performance. Currently, there is research into the use of disposable equipment in medical operations to try to reduce the risk of spreading some of the more resistant bacteria which are not destroyed by normal disinfection processes.

Scholarly research

This type of research is based around research which aims to expand current knowledge about a particular issue or topic. It is detailed and rigorous research which relies on the methodology being applied very thoroughly. Work is often published in specialist journals for the subject concerned. These journals provide useful up-to-date material for other researchers as it is generally 'cutting edge' information which cannot be found in textbooks.

> **EXAMPLE**
>
> Research into how children learn to read where methods are compared in terms of levels of success or how they learn though a newly developed technique may fit into this type of research.

Creative research

This involves research which develops and invents new images and items. This includes new designs of things. Although creativity can be found in many types of research, this type of research is specifically linked to the arts.

> **EXAMPLE**
>
> This type of research may be used when looking at the design of accommodation for people with physical impairments. It will focus on developing the type of environment which allows individuals to live as independent a life as possible. This may include developing items which will help them to carry out tasks with more ease.

Longitudinal research

This research takes place over a long period of time. It involves the researcher following the progress or development of something or someone. It aims to give a picture of changes over time rather than a one-off assessment of what is happening at one particular moment in time. Several of the different types of research mentioned above can fit into this category.

> **EXAMPLE**
>
> It may be used in a child study which looks at aspects of child development over a year.

How long does research take?

The length of a research programme will depend on many things, such as funding available and costs, time available and breadth of the study. However, the most important factor that will determine the length of the study will be the topic and the aim of the research – what do you want to find out?

Short studies

Some research has a very narrow focus and a limited time span and therefore will not take as long to carry out. The aim may be to find out what is happening here and now. Therefore, if the research takes place over too long a period, it will not be relevant in terms of the aims of the work.

Most student research will be short-term work as you do not have a lot of time in which to do the work and therefore your topic needs to be well focused to ensure it is realistic in terms of the time you have.

For example, If you have to complete your research project over three or four months, you couldn't, for example, realistically research how far the nursery provision in a town meets the needs of the working parents, but you could look at how far one particular nursery meets the needs of its parents.

Think about it

Look at the different types of research listed above.

◆ *Which do you think fit into longitudinal studies and which into short studies?*

◆ *Why do you think they fit as they do?*

◆ *Are there any which could easily fit both categories?*

◆ *Give examples of how this may happen.*

Types of research methods

There are two main ways of gathering information for a research project. You can either find out information for yourself or you can search out information that others have produced. Finding things out for yourself is known as **primary research**. Using material that others have produced is called **secondary research**, which is often the starting point for any research topic.

Secondary research

Carrying out secondary research means looking at material that has already been written on the topic you are researching. It is always wise to do this at the start of any research as it will give you an idea of the issues and thinking that are linked to your topic area. It may also give you some idea of the research methods you should be using when you start primary research; and it will also give you information to compare your findings with.

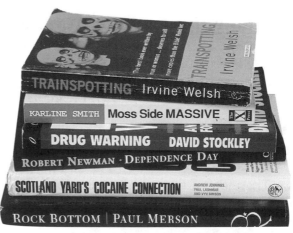

Secondary sources provide a wealth of information – newspapers and books are two examples of secondary sources

There are several sources of secondary information. These include books, government publications, statistics, the Internet, media sources such as newspapers, magazines and journals. Your topic will determine which of these is relevant for your study. There will usually be some secondary source material whatever your topic. However, for more up-to-date or current topics, the sources are likely to be journals or the Internet rather than textbooks – it can take up to a year for new information to get into textbooks.

It is likely that you will find others have carried out research in the area you are going to look at. It is common for several researchers to have carried out work in the same or similar areas. Repeating research can bring advances in thinking or understanding. It can also highlight new areas which need investigation.

You may be lucky and find a lot of published material on your chosen topic. The key will be to decide what is relevant and of value to your work. It will also be necessary to assess the quality of the information you have found. Just because it is printed does not mean it is accurate or correct. Look at how the information was collected and decide if you feel the material is good.

It is also worth remembering that information can be distorted, so look carefully. Using statistics is one way researchers do this. For example, a researcher may report their findings on use of disposable nappies as indicating that 80% of mothers use disposable nappies, which is a significant number and a major finding. However, if the sample used was only 10 mothers and the 80% was actually eight out of ten, then it isn't quite so credible.

You also need to consider the research methods used to gain the information. If the research methods have not been carried out rigorously – that is, thoroughly and accurately – then the results and subsequent information will not be valid.

Assessing secondary sources of information is not always easy.

Primary research methods

Primary research involves you collecting your own data using one of the primary research techniques.

Primary research methods include questionnaires, interviews, observations, analysis of books or statistics, surveys and experiments. The primary research methods that you choose will depend on your topic and what you are hoping to find out. All of the primary research methods need careful planning if they are to produce information which is valid and reliable.

Primary research methods can be either quantitative or qualitative. Raw data collected by others but not analysed can also be classed as primary research.

Quantitative and qualitative research methods

Quantitative

Quantitative research methods produce data which can be analysed statistically. They usually generate large quantities of information and sample sizes are usually big. The most effective way to handle and make sense of such information is through mathematical manipulation or statistics. The use of statistics to analyse the information means that a lot of information can be presented in a manageable format.

Generally, the information is presented using graphs, charts and diagrams. In this way the reader easily gets an overview of the findings and can quickly see patterns.

Questionnaires and data collection surveys are generally considered quantitative research methods as they seek information from large numbers of people. In order to handle the large amount of data, most researchers would design questionnaires and surveys with questions with a choice of specified answers. The responses are most effectively analysed in the form of statistics.

Qualitative

Qualitative research methods tend to aim for depth of response rather than high numbers of respondents. Therefore, this method of research is interested in people's attitudes, opinions and thoughts on issues. The methods allow the researcher to understand the situation more, so they can begin to make sense of it.

This type of information cannot be easily analysed in a mathematical way and therefore cannot usually be converted into statistics. Much of the quality and meaning of responses would be lost by doing this. Therefore, the information is used to support arguments or points and often quoted verbatim (exactly as it has been said to the researcher).

Examples of qualitative research methods are interviews and observations.

Both types of research provide valuable information. The choice of which ones to use will depend on the topic being researched and the aims of that research. Good research generally uses both types as this can help provide balance in the work.

Triangulation

Triangulation is an important concept in research. It involves the researcher using at least three methods to collect data on a topic – for example, secondary research, questionnaires and interviews. This is to try to show similarities and findings across a range of research methods so as to support the validity and reliability of the work.

Ethics in research

Research often involves people and finding out information about them. It is important to consider the 'rights' of the person involved in the research before you carry it out. This means maintaining the confidentiality and anonymity of the people you use in your research. This is known as **ethics**.

Ethics are about human behaviour. They involve considering whether the way something is carried out is right or wrong, and this includes whether the behaviour is morally right. They consider the effects that someone's actions have on others.

The *Collins Concise Dictionary* (1995) defines ethics as:

the philosophical study of the moral value of human conduct and the rules and principles that ought to govern it

Ethics are used as a guideline to making decisions. Everyone has a set of ethics – i.e. what they believe is right and wrong. These may differ to some extent from person to person, but in any particular society they will broadly be the same. They are based on the values we are brought up with and they will influence our behaviour and attitude, as well as our conscience.

Ethics are based on attitudes, values and beliefs and therefore cannot be measured. They are conceptual, i.e. formed in the mind. Below are definitions of some words to help you understand what ethics are in more depth.

Sometimes people are described as having old-fashioned values. What does this mean?

Can you give an example?

Definitions

Attitude

In a research context, attitude means the views or opinions of an individual towards an issue or topic. These views may be positive or negative.

Values

This applies to the beliefs and accepted standards of behaviour within a social grouping.

Values are principles or personal rules or standards which enable people to make decisions and choose between alternatives. Values influence behaviour and guide people into choosing appropriate behaviour in different circumstances.

Beliefs

An individual's beliefs are based on the information and knowledge they have about the world. They are something that an individual accepts as true or real, i.e. they are personal opinion. Different people will have different beliefs, just as they have a different experience of the world.

Do you have any personal attitudes, values or beliefs which you follow when living your life?

Look at the three statements listed below. Do you agree or disagree with them?

◆ *Women should stay at home with their children.*

◆ *The police should tell local people when a convicted child molester moves into their area.*

◆ *People who smack their children should be prosecuted.*

Discuss the statements as a group.

Did you notice any differences in the attitudes or values of members of the group?

Applying ethics when carrying out research

In all aspects of research, ethics can be applied to the way the research methods are carried out. They will influence what is considered to be good or bad practice in the methodology. Ethics also apply to the way the information that has been gathered is used.

Anyone who carries out research needs to think about the ethical issues which affect the work being carried out. It means taking a responsible attitude to the work you are doing and the results you get. Often, people will give you personal and sensitive information about some matter, therefore they and the information should be treated with respect and in confidence. Remember that different people have different opinions on what is sensitive information, so the best approach is to treat any information which is given to you in any research method as confidential. Do not repeat that information to anyone in a form which can be traced back to the person who gave it.

There are ways of giving out information without breaking the confidentiality of the source

It is important that people who give information in the research process give their **informed consent** for its use. This means that they fully understand what they are agreeing to take part in.

People involved in research have a right to know how the information being collected about them will be used. Permission may be needed before some information can be collected, especially if the research involves obtaining information from children, people with special needs or from a particular organisation or establishment.

Confidentiality is another important issue to be aware of. All information collected through different primary research methods should be confidential. Therefore, it is important that you do not discuss with family or friends any specific details of what individuals have said or put in questionnaires. This is easy to do when chatting casually, but you could find yourself in difficulties if you were overheard or if someone repeated your comments. People are bound to be interested in what you are doing, so you should be prepared to give an overview or general findings but not to attribute comments to individuals.

All research should show an awareness of culture, race, family circumstance, gender, disability, age and sexual orientation. Respect for others includes respect for their customs and beliefs.

In order to maintain confidentiality, it is important that the participants, that is the people you use in your research, remain anonymous. This can be achieved by changing the names or using codes, for example by referring to the people used as participant one, participant two, participant three, and so on.

Data Protection Act 1998

The Data Protection Act 1998 came into force on the 1 March 2000. It is an important law as it gives priority to personal privacy and protection of personal information in a way that did not exist before. The Act covers both fact and opinions on individuals that may be kept on record. It also increases the individual's rights to access any information which organisations might be keeping on them.

Everyone has to comply with the Act. Anyone who wants to collect personal data must say how the information will be used and who the information may be given to in the process of using it. In some cases, such as educational establishments, individuals have to give their permission for personal information to be used.

The Act requires people collecting data to follow some principles of good practice. These are:

◆ Data must be fairly and lawfully processed.

◆ Data must be processed for limited purposes only.

◆ Data recorded must be adequate, relevant, but not excessive.

◆ Data recorded must be accurate.

◆ Data should not be kept longer than necessary.

◆ Data must be processed in accordance with data subjects' rights.

◆ Data must be kept in a secure place.

◆ Data should not be transferred to another country without adequate protection.

From a research point of view, you need to be aware of the implications of the Data Protection Act, as to how it affects the information you collect as part of the research process and what you do with it. You need to make sure you collect only information that is essential for the work you are carrying out and that you store any information carefully. Make sure that you do not pass on any information to others without the permission of the individual. Do not store material any longer than necessary.

ACTIVITY

How much do you now understand about research?
Give a definition of each of the terms listed below:
1 Research
2 Methodology
3 Ethics
4 Sampling
5 Qualitative
6 Quantitative
7 Survey
8 Secondary research
9 Primary research
10 Longitudinal studies

Answers to Test

1 A way in which new things are found out.

2 The study of the research techniques which may be used.

3 Something that influences the way the research is carried out – ensuring it is morally correct.

4 Sampling is the decision about who you are going to use in your research and how many people.

5 Research methods which get personal views and opinions from people. They generate a lot of information rather than figures.

6 Research methods which tend to produce a lot of numbers and statistics. They do not tend to be in-depth research methods.

7 An umbrella term for questionnaires, interviews and data collection surveys.

8 Research which draws on material which has been written and/or published by someone else.

9 Research which is first-hand to the researchers, i.e. something they carry out themselves.

10 A study which goes on over a period of time, for example one year.

Further reading

Bell, J (1999) *Doing your research project,* Open University Press, Buckingham
Green, S (2000) *Research methods,* Stanley Thornes, Cheltenham
Tassoni, P and Beith, K (2000) *Diploma in child care and education,* Heinemann, Oxford

Useful websites

Data Protection Act – http://www.manches.co.uk
Data Protection Act – http://dataprotection.gov.uk

2 Analysing and presenting data

The last chapter explained the basics of the research process. Another important aspect of research is the way the information or data that you collect through the research process can be presented. Researchers need to be aware of this before they start the process as it can influence the way in which data is collected.

There are several different ways of presenting data and the one you choose will depend on the research method you have chosen and the results you have gained. The presentation of the results can help the reader to see patterns more easily.

This chapter covers:

◆ What is data?

◆ How should raw data be presented?

◆ Tables

◆ Calculating data – basic statistics

◆ Presenting information

◆ Using computers to calculate data and present results.

What is data?

Your research will produce large amounts of information. This is known as data. If you have chosen to use quantitative data, a lot of the information will be in a numerical format. You will need to make sense of this information. You can present the information in a text-based format, but using some form of numbers to depict the information will have more effect. This is usually achieved by presenting the information in the form of graphs, pie charts or diagrams.

The raw data is not usually presented as part of the finished project. It will be used to collate results and to decide how the results are best presented in the finished work. It is therefore important that you store any results in a logical and organised manner to help this process.

Although the raw data is not used in the report, it is usually retained for a period of time once the work is complete as a source of information in case any of the findings are questioned. It is therefore important that the data is kept in a format which is easy to retrieve for this purpose. It may be worth keeping it as a special file, sectioned according to the research method. This will help ensure that none of the material or rough work is lost.

How should raw data be presented?

Looking at a report on a piece of research, often you see a number of tables or graphs giving the information in an easy-to-read format. This style of presentation makes the results more accessible for the reader. Charts and graphs can present detailed information in a clear and concise format.

Different ways that data could be presented include:

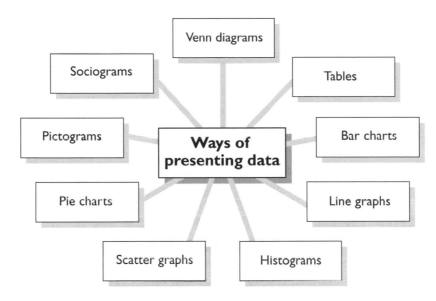

The choice of presentation is often a personal one. You can often present the same information in a variety of formats. You will need to decide which one presents your findings in the clearest manner. The rest of the chapter looks at the different methods of presentation to help you decide which ones you prefer to use.

You should be aware that charts and graphs can misrepresent the data, therefore it is important that you choose your form of presentation carefully.

Tables

A table is a way of presenting a range of information in a neat format. It can be a very useful way of presenting information if you want to compare data. For example, the following information shows the number of students on different courses over the past five years.

Course	1995	1996	1997	1998	1999	2000
DNN/Diploma in child care and education	20	18	16	14	14	15
GNVQ AVCE HSC	32	26	18	16	17	15
GNVQ Int HSC	15	10	9	8	9	10
BTEC National Early Years	10	15	18	18	18	20
NVQ Care		12	15	18	22	26
NVQ Early Years	8	15	20	20	24	28

You can use this information to draw a number of conclusions, such as which courses are growing and which are declining. You could further analyse the information by age to see if this affects the patterns of enrolments.

Setting out the information in this format makes it easier to see patterns emerging.

Tables must be clearly labelled so the reader can see what is being depicted. This includes the columns of information and giving the tables an overall title. If figures are being used, the units of measurement must be clear. If there is a lot of information in the table, colour coding can help the reader to access the information more easily.

In a group setting, collect information about the individuals present. Try not to make it too personal. Choose about five different pieces of information, such as shoe size, hair colour, eye colour, height, age.

Devise a chart to put your data into.

Calculating data – basic statistics

You can draw more conclusions from raw data if you analyse it through different calculations. The most common ones are the mean, mode, median and range.

The following data on children's shoe sizes will be used to illustrate each of the techniques.

The shoe sizes were measured for a group of Year 2 children:

10	12	11	11	13	9	12	13	10	11	10	9
11	12	11	11	9							

Mean

The mean is the average of the group of data collected. To calculate the mean, all the figures in the data set need to be added together and then divided by the number in the sample.

This will give you the average figure for the data, or the *mean*.

10+12+11+11+13+9+12+13+10+11+10+9+11+12+11+11+9 = 185
185 divided by 17 = 10.9

Therefore the mean shoe size is 10.9.

Mode

The mode is the figure that appears the most times in a set of data. It is the most common figure. To calculate the mode, you need to list how many times each figure appears, as in the following:

Size 9	3
Size 10	3
Size 11	6
Size 12	3
Size 13	2

Therefore, the most common shoe size, the *mode*, is size 11.

Sometimes more than one number appears the same number of times. For example, if the data for shoe sizes were as follows:

Size 9	3
Size 10	3
Size 11	6
Size 12	6
Size 13	2

In this example, two sizes appear the most frequently – sizes 11 and 12. In this case, both would be the mode. This is known as bi-modal because there are two numbers the same.

Tri-modal is also possible, where three figures appear the same number of times.

Median

The median is the figure that falls in the middle of a set of data when listed from the lowest to the highest figure. It is the middle value. The easiest way to find the median is to order the figures from the lowest to the highest.

| 9 | 9 | 9 | 10 | 10 | 10 | 11 | 11 | (11) | 11 | 11 | 11 |
| | 12 | 12 | 12 | 13 | 13 | | | | | | |

Size 11 is the one that falls in the middle, and it is therefore the *median* value. There are eight values either side of (11), making it the middle of the data set.

If you have an even number in the data set, you will find that the median falls between two figures. For example:

| 9 | 9 | 10 | 10 | 11 | (11 | 12) | 12 | 13 | 13 | 13 | 13 |

In this situation, the median is the sum of the two numbers divided by 2. For example:

11 + 12 = 23
23 divided by 2 = 11.5

Therefore, the median is 11.5.

Range

The range is the difference between the highest and lowest figure in the data set. To find the range, you subtract the lowest figure from the highest.

13 − 9 = 4

Therefore, the range is 4.

The interquartile range is the difference between the first and third quartiles. This removes numbers which are unusually large or small from the range.

Standard deviation

If data is normally distributed or is close to normal, variability can be best shown through standard deviation. Standard deviation is an indication of how widely the data collected is distributed across the range and can show how widely the data is spread from the mean. To calculate the standard deviation, you take the mean of the set of data as the central point and look at how far the results spread either side of the mean.

For example, the ages of the six members of the Jones family are 2, 4, 6, 8, 31 and 33. The mean age is 14.

The deviation from the mean is found by subtracting the mean from each value.

Age	Mean	Deviation
2	14	−12
4	14	−10
6	14	−8
8	14	−6
31	14	17
33	14	19

A small standard deviation would see all the results in a narrow band around the mean, whereas a large standard deviation would have a broader spread away from the mean.

Sometimes data will be higher than the mean and this will give a positive number. Other data may be lower than the mean and so produce a negative figure.

If you add all the standard deviations together, the result should be zero, as this is how the mean is defined.

To give positive numbers to work on, the deviations from the mean are squared before being added together.

In a standard deviation, fixed proportions of the curve fall within standard deviations of the mean. Approximately 68% of any population should be within one standard deviation of the mean – that is, 34% either side. You would expect to find 96% of the population within two standard deviations. Therefore, a typical standard deviation curve would look as follows:

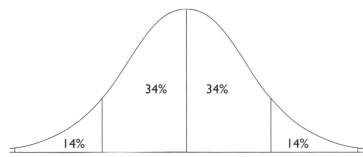

34%   34%

14%   14%

This information allows you to make future predictions

Grouping data

Another way of organising data is to divide it into groups and create a grouped frequency table from the set of data. If you decide to do this, it is important that you choose a suitable class interval to use. You can do this by finding the range of the data that you have collected and then deciding what the suitable intervals might be.

If you were looking at the ages of people who attended a day centre, you might collect data as follows:

| 56 | 65 | 73 | 92 | 83 | 73 | 79 | 68 | 59 | 64 | 74 | 68 |
| 91 | 89 | 77 | 69 | 66 | 64 | 72 | 73 | 85 | 94 | 66 | 88 |

The range of ages is from 56 to 94. Using a class interval of 5 years will give you eight intervals see below.

Class interval	Tally	Cumulative
56–60	II	2
61–65	III	5
66–70	IIIII	10
71–75	IIIII	15
76–80	II	17
81–85	II	19
86–90	II	21
91–95	III	24

A grouping like this shows how the ages are distributed. You could decide to use wider intervals but this would not show the spread of ages as effectively. Smaller intervals would not show any meaningful information as there would be too few pieces of data in each interval.

The cumulative frequency column on the chart allows you to see very quickly the age profile of the clients. For example, it shows that 19 of the 24 clients are under 85 years of age.

Presenting information

Most research projects will require you to present data in a pictorial format. This is generally in the form of a bar chart, histogram, line graph, pie chart or pictogram.

Graphs

There are various types of graphs which can be used to present data. The type you choose will depend on the type of data you wish to present. There are a number of important points you need to remember whatever type of graph you use.

◆ Graphs generally have both vertical and horizontal axes.

◆ The axes should be clearly labelled, explaining what each one represents.

◆ If you are using units of measurement, make sure it is clear what they are.

◆ All graphs should have a clear title which informs the reader what the graph is about.

◆ Graphs should be presented on graph paper, not on lined paper.

◆ Pie charts should be presented only on plain paper, not on lined or graph paper.

◆ The source of any data used must be given on the graph – this is usually in small writing at the bottom.

Bar charts

The most common type of graph used is a bar chart. This is because they are easy to draw and easy to understand. They are useful for presenting data for descriptive categories, such as the number of children attending different types of childcare, or for specific grouped data, such as the age of students studying health and social care courses in a college.

On bar charts, the bars may be close together or have a space between each one. Bar charts have a number of common features. These are:

◆ All bars are the same width.

◆ Bars may be horizontal or vertical.

◆ The length of the bar indicates the frequency.

◆ Only one axis has a scale: the other has discrete or descriptive categories, such as months of the year, days of the week, colours, type of pre-school provision, etc.

◆ Bar charts are often coloured to enhance the presentation.

◆ Codes may be used to label the bars but the key must be included on the graph and clearly show what each is.

Line graphs

This is another type of graph which is often used when changes over time need to be presented. A line graph can show very clearly fluctuations in values. Generally, you need a lot of data to be able to produce a meaningful line graph. Limited information will result in a graph which gives the wrong impression.

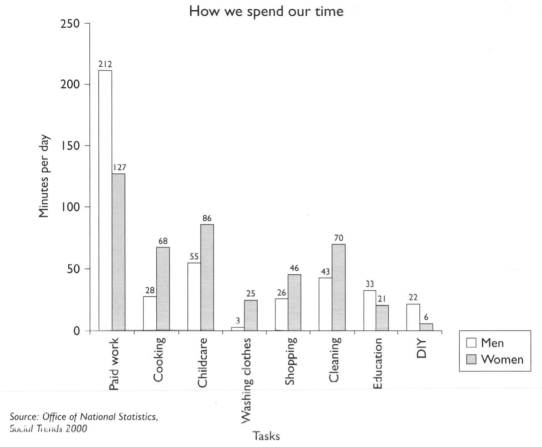

Source: Office of National Statistics,
Social Trends 2000

A bar chart

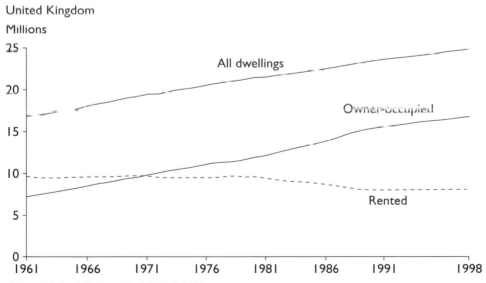

Source: Office of National Statistics, Social Trends 2000

A line graph

The graph is produced by plotting the points of data on the graph and then joining them up to produce a line.

Common features of line graphs are:

◆ The horizontal axis has a continuous variable such as age, time, temperature or number.

◆ The vertical axis has the scale.

◆ Good for plotting more than one line on a graph to show differences, for example population growth of two different countries over a 50-year period.

Histograms

Histograms can look very similar to bar charts, but there are a number of major differences.

◆ Histograms are generally used for grouped data.

◆ The columns are not all the same width. They vary according to the proportion of the size or class they represent.

◆ There are no gaps between the columns.

◆ The frequency of the class is indicated by the size of the column.

◆ The horizontal axis has a scale similar to any other graph in that each interval represents the same number of units.

Using the data on the ages of clients in a day centre, a histogram to depict that information would be calculated as follows:

Class interval (yrs)	Frequency	Frequency density
56–60	2	0.03
61–65	3	0.04
66–70	5	0.07
71–75	5	0.06
76–80	2	0.02
81–85	2	0.02
86–90	2	0.02
91–95	3	0.03

The first task you need to do is to calculate the height and width of the columns on the histogram.

The width will be the class interval, e.g. 56–60, 61–65, and so on.

The height or frequency density is calculated by dividing the frequency by the width. Therefore, the sum is:

$$\text{Height (frequency density)} = \frac{\text{frequency}}{\text{class interval}}$$

This means $\dfrac{2}{60} = 0.03$

The histogram will look like this:

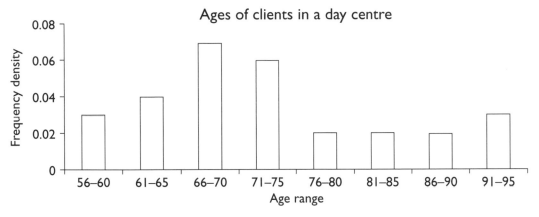

Histogram showing age range of 56–95

Interpreting histograms

If all the columns are the same width as with the histogram above, you can easily interpret the histogram by comparing the height of each column. However, if the columns are different widths, you will need to calculate the area of each column in order to be able to draw conclusions.

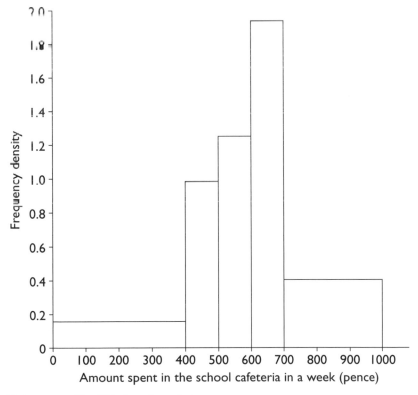

Histogram with differing size columns

Scatter graphs

Another frequently used graph is a scatter graph. Scatter graphs are generally used when you need to present data showing two corresponding variables, for example height and weight, GCSE score and Advanced level results, or blood pressure and age. This type of graph can help you to see patterns that may emerge as a result of the two variables being linked together.

For example, the blood pressure of a number of pregnant women was taken at the same stage of pregnancy. The women were of varying ages. The results were as follows:

| **Age:** | 23 | 18 | 34 | 41 | 29 | 27 | 31 | 17 | 20 | 22 | 27 |
| **BP:** | 70 | 65 | 75 | 85 | 74 | 78 | 80 | 67 | 69 | 71 | 73 |

Presenting this data as a scatter graph would very quickly show if there was any correlation between blood pressure and age in this group of women.

It is important to note that a correlation does not always mean cause and effect. The data may show a correlation such as the older the woman the higher the blood pressure but this does not mean that this will be the case with all women. Other factors, such as exercise levels or stress levels, could be influencing the pattern you have identified. You could have a cohort of women in highly pressurised jobs. If you carried out the test on a group of women across the age range who did not work, the pattern of results might be very different.

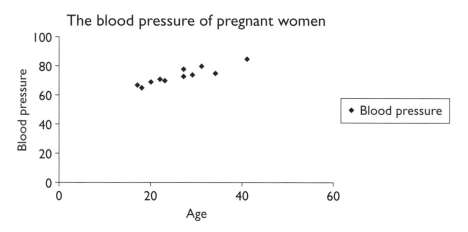

Scatter graph showing the blood pressure of pregnant women

To interpret the graph, you are looking for a pattern or correlation which suggests that changes in one variable have an effect on the other. This correlation could be positive or negative or show that there is little or no relationship between the two variables.

The three graphs opposite show positive, negative and no correlation.

Graph 1 shows a positive correlation. This clearly shows that there is a strong link between the two variables, and that as one increases, so does the other.

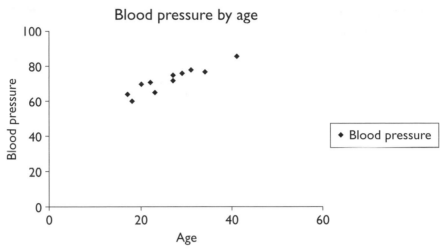

Graph 2 demonstrates a negative correlation. In this case, it suggests that there is a link between the two variables, but as one increases, the other decreases.

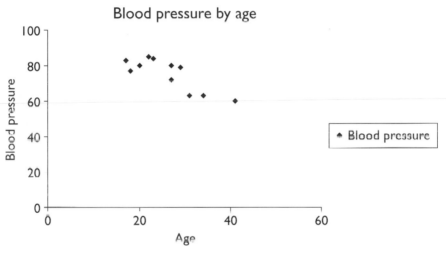

Graph 3 shows little or no correlation as the points are spread across the graph and there is no clear pattern to speak of.

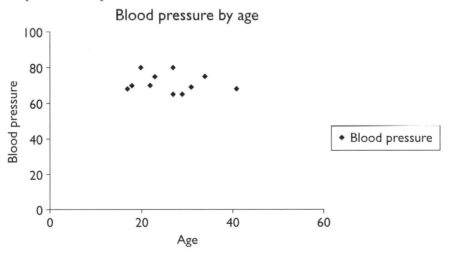

When you have produced a scatter graph, it is useful to draw in *a line of best fit*. A line of best fit is where you draw a line, using a ruler, in the area where there is a cluster of points. This will give the appearance of the points being clustered around the line. This line can then be used as a starting point for devising a formula to link the two values. This formula is then used to make predictions of one value, given the value of another.

Therefore, using this formula, you should be able to predict, for example, what the blood pressure might be for a 43-year-old pregnant woman, as well as that for a 16-year-old.

Pie charts

Pie charts are a way of presenting the data collected by each category's share of the total. The figures have first to be converted into percentages in order to do this.

A simple way to find the percentage is to divide the component by the total and then multiply by 100.

Once you have calculated the percentages, you need to convert this into degrees in order to construct the pie chart.

For example, imagine you collected data on the way in which the staff in a health centre travel to work, and the results were as follows:

Form of travel	Number of people	%	Degrees
Public transport (bus)	10	17	61
Public transport (train)	4	7	25
Walk	15	25	90
By car	25	43	155
Bicycle	3	5	18
Motor cycle	2	3	11
Total	59	100	360

To work out the percentage for each form of travel, you would do the following:

Public transport (bus) $\dfrac{10}{59}$ = 0.17 (rounded to 2 decimal places)

Total no. of people $0.17 \times 100 = 17\%$

To find the degrees each section takes of the pie, you divide 360 degrees by 100, which equals 3.6 degrees per percent. You then multiply the percentage of each section by 3.6.

$17 \times 3.6 = 61$ degrees

Therefore, public transport (bus) would be represented by 61 degrees of the pie chart.

The pie chart would look as follows:

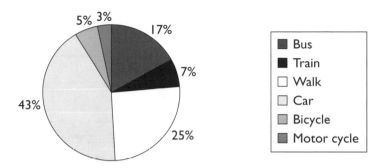

Methods used by health centre staff to travel to work

- Bus
- Train
- Walk
- Car
- Bicycle
- Motor cycle

5% 3% 17% 7% 25% 43%

A pie chart

Remember to:

◆ show your calculations

◆ colour each segment to improve the presentation

◆ give each section a label

◆ include a clear key on the diagram, especially if the sections are too small to label clearly

◆ give the pie chart a clear title

◆ present your pie chart on plain paper.

Sociograms

A sociogram is a good way of showing a social structure. Sociograms are used to depict the relationships between different members of a group. They can clearly show the relationships between each member of a group, or, alternatively, they can show the relationships of one specific group member.

A sociogram looks something like a bar chart with horizontal bars. The names of all the people in the group are listed on the right-hand axis and frequency is across the bottom axis. This allows you to depict the number of times a person is mentioned as a 'friend' of another person.

The sociogram could also be designed to give the names of the people who mentioned a particular name. This would allow you to see if there is any pattern developing. It would be common for a pattern to be established with older children or adults as they tend to form more stable friendship groups than younger children.

The results of a sociogram where you ask a child in Year 1 to name his or her three best friends in class might look as follows (see overleaf).

Name	Friend	Friend	Friend
Jane	Marsha	Ali	Jo
Ben	Tim	Mark	James
Tim	Mark	Ben	
Marsha	Jane	Laura	Jo
Laura	Ali	Jo	Jane
Steven	James	Mark	Tim
Jo	Jane	Gill	Laura

Friendship groups in the Year 1 class

This could then be converted into a graph which shows the frequency at which each individual child has been named.

As with other graphs and charts, the sociogram should be clearly labelled. This includes labelling both axes and giving the chart a clear title.

Venn diagrams

A Venn diagram is a good way of showing interaction between individuals or different groups of people. A Venn diagram consists of circles which interlink, and therefore suggest areas of overlap or common ground.

For example, a day centre has a number of clients who stay for lunch. They each have different needs.

Clients who stay for lunch	Clients who need help to eat	Clients who need soft food	Clients who need a diabetic diet
Jane	Jane	Buster	Amy
Buster	James	Julie	Julie
James	Amy	Amy	James
Julie			Jim
Jim			
Amy			

This is represented in the following way by a Venn diagram:

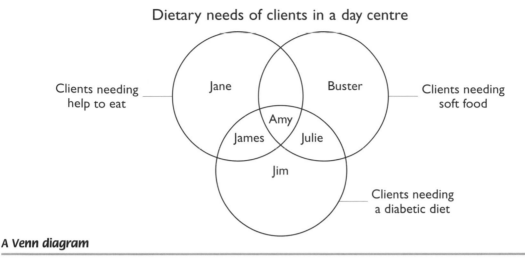

Dietary needs of clients in a day centre

Clients needing help to eat — Jane

Buster — Clients needing soft food

Amy

James Julie

Jim

Clients needing a diabetic diet

A Venn diagram

The Venn diagram shows that Amy is the only client who is diabetic, needs soft food and help to eat.

Pictograms

A pictogram is a way of depicting data in a pictorial format. It often uses pictures or symbols to show information, rather than lines or bars. The finished pictogram is usually presented in a row or a column. It can be a very creative way of showing results.

Used carefully, with thought, a pictogram can be very attractive and give a bold impression.

An example of a pictogram showing the different eye colours of children in a nursery class is given below.

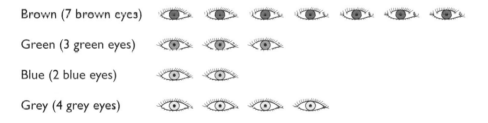

Brown (7 brown eyes)

Green (3 green eyes)

Blue (2 blue eyes)

Grey (4 grey eyes)

The different eye colours in Year 1

Sources of error

Errors can affect the research process at a number of different stages in the process. They can occur at the data collection stage, perhaps through low response rates or as a result of interviewer/interviewee interaction. Interviewer bias can be a common factor that affects results. Bias means that the views or opinions of the interviewer have influenced the way they have carried out their research methodology. Bias during the interview process is explained in more detail in Chapter 7.

Errors may also result from the actual research collection tools themselves, through inappropriate questions or questions that have been misunderstood. Many of these errors can be eliminated through carefully planning and trialing of the research tool to be used.

Errors can also occur when analysing the data. Errors in calculation are possible, therefore it is wise to estimate what you think the results should look like and double-check before finally completing any graphs or charts.

It is also common for errors to occur in the way statistics are used. Correlations are easy to find but can be far more difficult to explain. You need to be careful when you are interpreting the data that you report only what you see and can be sure about. What appears to be a clear correlation between two factors may be happening because of a third, unregistered, factor.

Extrapolation can be another common error, where you try to predict patterns beyond the results you have gained. It is important that you comment only on the results you have gained for the data you have collected. Broad and wild predictions are likely to be inaccurate and would make your research project invalid.

Sources of error will occur in most research projects. You need to try to be as accurate as you can at each stage of the process. It is wise to check and double-check all aspects of the process, from the trial of methods to the calculations based on the data. Above all, be honest about shortcomings and potential errors in your evaluation.

Using computers to calculate data and present results

It is becoming increasingly common for researchers to use computer programs to help them analyse and present data. Computer programs have the advantage of being able to calculate accurately, provided the information is inputted accurately in the first place. They are also able to present the data very professionally and can show the data in a range of formats at the touch of a button, allowing the researcher to select the best format with ease.

Above all, once the data has been inputted, the production of the graphs and charts is very quick. One of the most common packages to use for data analysis is the Excel package.

Using Excel

Excel is a spreadsheet package available as part of the Microsoft® Office package on many computers. Excel can help you to present data effectively. It will also convert the information into graphs at the touch of a button!

A spreadsheet is designed for working with numerical information. Therefore it is useful when collating quantitative data, as in the case of questionnaires from which numerical information will be generated. The information on a spreadsheet is organised into rows and columns. An Excel spreadsheet appears on screen looking like this:

	A	B	C	D	E	F
1						
2						
3						
4						
5						

There are over 200 rows on the page of a spreadsheet and over 60 columns, so there should be plenty of space to present even the most complicated information.

The spreadsheet is made up of lots of individual cells which are identified on most spreadsheets with a letter and a number. For example A1 is a cell, E4 is a cell, and so on. This is known as the cell reference. You can use the cursor to move from one cell to another. As you highlight the cell, the cell becomes active and you can put information into that cell.

You will not be able to see the whole of the spreadsheet at once as the computer cannot display all the information on the screen. As you use the arrow keys and the bottom or side of the page, more of the spreadsheet will come into view.

Using formulae

You can use mathematical formulae as part of the spreadsheet to give automatic calculations.

A formula is written in an active cell. It will then carry out the calculation as instructed and put the result in that cell.

The symbols used for this are:

+   for add
−   for subtract
*   for multiply
/   for divide
=   for equals
()   for defining the sum.

When used in formulae, these symbols are known as mathematical operators.

Writing formulae

	A	B	C	D
1	3	4	=A1+B1	
2				
3				
4				

If you wanted cell C1 to be the total of A1 and B1, you write the formula =A1+B1 in cell C1. The = sign tells the computer that you are writing a formula. This will appear in the cell itself and in the box at the top of the spreadsheet, until you press the return key which will then activate the formula.

The spreadsheet will look as follows:

	A	B	C	D
1	3	4	7	
2				
3				
4				

Once the formula is inserted in the cell, it will automatically recalculate the sum if any of the other figures vary.

If you want to add the information in more than two cells, you can make a long formula, e.g. = A2 + B2 + C2 + D2, or use the command SUM (A2:D2). This will add all the rows from A2 to D2.

Copying formulae

Once you have written the correct formula in a cell, it is possible to copy it into another cell by using the copy and paste command on the formula bar. If you copied the formula in cell E2 to cell E3, it would convert the formula to be the SUM (A3:D3). Cell references which are able to change in this way are known as **relative cell references**.

You can also fix the cell so that the computer does not change the formula as it is copied into another cell. This is known as an **absolute cell reference**. The symbol $ is used to depict an absolute cell.

Producing graphs and diagrams from a spreadsheet

Once all the data has been inputted on to the spreadsheet, it is relatively easy to produce graphs and diagrams. To do this, you need to highlight the required section on the spreadsheet and instruct the spreadsheet to reproduce the data as the type of chart you require. The examples below show how the same data can be presented in different formats using Excel. This data has already been shown as an example of a pie chart earlier in the chapter.

A pie chart showing the way health centre staff travel to work

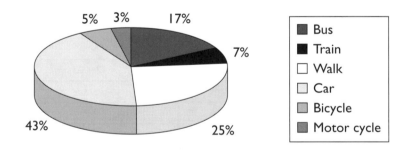

A chart showing how people travel to work at a health centre

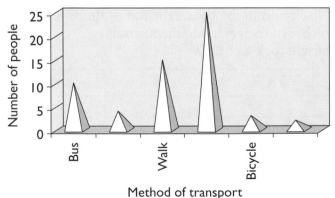

A bar chart showing how people travel to work at a health centre

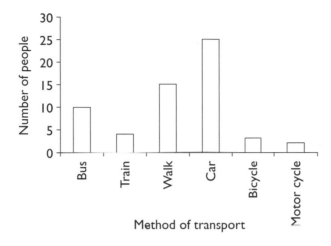

Charts

As with any other charts and graphs, it is important that you label these clearly and accurately. In many cases, the key will be automatically produced on the chart or graph by the computer.

- *Using the information you collected on children in a group, put the information into a spreadsheet*
- *Select one aspect and print off the data in at least two types of chart or graph.*
- *Which depicts the data most appropriately and why?*
- *What are the advantages of using a computer package to generate these charts?*

Further reading

Rowntree, D (1991) *Statistics without tears*, Penguin, London
Any GCSE mathematics study guide.

Useful websites

www.statistics.gov.uk
www.stats.gla.ac.uk

ACTIVITY

Jemima has carried out a data collection survey on shopping habits of people in wheelchairs. She chose to sample 20 wheelchair-bound people who live on their own. Her aim was to find out about the issues they face when trying to do their weekly food shop. Her results were as follows:

a   Five used their own car to shop.

b   Five were taken shopping by a relative.

c   Four went shopping with friends.

d   Six had a home help who did their shopping for them.

◆   Of the nine people in **b** and **c**, six went with others because they needed help with their shopping.

◆   Of the five in **a**, two needed help going around the supermarket and packing.

◆   All 14 in **a**, **b**, and **c** needed help taking the shopping to the car.

◆   Three people in **d** did a limited amount of shopping in their local shops.

Questions

1   What do you think is the best way for Jemima to present the findings?

2   Why have you chosen this method?

3   Present the information as a

   Bar chart

   Pie chart

   Pictogram.

   Which do you think presents the information most effectively?

4   What other information do you think Jemima could have found out to extend the work?

PART **2**

Secondary research methods

3 Doing a literature search

The quality of the literature search can greatly affect the quality of the investigation. A good literature search can help ensure a research project is focused and relevant. It informs the whole piece of work and is therefore extremely important. A poor literature search can result in the investigation being badly informed and without a clear focus.

In this chapter, we look at the different literature sources and explore how they can be used to inform the whole investigation. The chapter will cover:

◆ Secondary sources

◆ Using books

◆ How many books should be used in a literature search?

◆ Cleaning information

◆ Acknowledging your sources

◆ Being up to date

◆ Being critical about books

◆ What to do when there is limited published material

◆ Using documents as a source of information

◆ Reports

◆ Minutes as part of 'documents'

◆ Using promotional material

◆ Research using the Internet.

Secondary sources

There is a wide range of information already published in secondary source material that anyone researching a topic can draw on. It is important to begin any research project with an explanation of the secondary source material that is available on the topic. This will give background information, which will help the researcher understand:

◆ The research that has previously been done on the topic.

◆ The theories that already exist in relation to the topic.

Secondary source material includes books, documents, maps and CD-ROMs. Information on the Internet is also a secondary source.

   Information from all secondary sources will help in the design of interviews and questionnaires, as well as providing something to compare the findings against. The skill for researchers will be in selecting the relevant material for their study. They will also need to identify connections or patterns which they would wish to explore further. The secondary source material may also give explanations which could be tested through the study. For example, if you were doing an investigation into adolescent eating habits, you might find out through secondary research that adolescents tend to miss breakfast. You could then use questionnaires and interviews as a means of testing if this is true, with the people you use in your research.

Using books

Books can be used in a number of ways to support a research project.

Using books as a source of data/information (secondary research)

Information from books can provide background or understanding of the context in which the research project sits. It may give an overview of broader issues surrounding the topic or an indication of trends or patterns linked to it. This is the most common use of books in research.

   More importantly, the background research will give researchers the understanding and information they need to be able to compare, analyse and evaluate their findings. It will allow them to set the results in the context of the topic as a whole, and in doing so to increase the validity of the work.

   Research can give an historical perspective on the topic chosen. It may be able to highlight changes over a period of time. For example, if you are researching into divorce patterns in the UK, you may find that the divorce rate has increased over the years. Background research into divorce and the law will show that divorce law changed in the 1986, which made divorce easier. So, this can help explain why the rate of divorce has increased since that date.

Using books as a source of ideas

Books, such as this book on research methods, can give help and guidance when planning and carrying out a research project. They are a source of ideas, which may be imitated or developed. They can also give details about how to do a research project and the relative merits of different research methods.

Such texts help researchers to avoid problems as they carry out their research. When used as a guide, they can help ensure the work is carried out in such a way as to be valid and reliable. The value of such a textbook tends to be greatest at the beginning of the study as it helps the researcher to plan what he or she intends to do.

Using books for primary research

Books themselves can be used as a primary research method. This occurs when the books themselves are the source of the research and are analysed in some way. An example might be analysing the representation of different cultures in children's storybooks.

How you might design and carry out a book analysis is covered later in Chapter 9.

Using books as a source of information

As most research projects will use books to support findings, it is worthwhile exploring some guidelines for this.

Doing the literature search

Initially, a researcher needs to identify the material that is available on a topic.

The first stage in this process would be to identify the section in the library which is likely to contain textbooks on the topic. Libraries are generally organised according to the Dewey system, a numbering system which allows texts to be categorised according to topic.

The Dewey system is a three-digit numbering system, e.g. 304 or 501. Each three-figure number represents a major category. These are further broken down by adding decimal places, e.g. 304.412 or 501.2, which allow for more specific classifications. The decimal figures will cover texts which are close to the main categories. This makes it far easier to locate the exact book that you want. In most libraries, the ends of the shelves are labelled with the main categories to help readers locate the appropriate section. Having identified the appropriate sections, texts either side of the number may be of interest as well, as they may be related.

Example of the Dewey system:

300 – Social sciences
301 – Sociology and anthropology
302 – Social interaction
303 – Social processes
304 – Factors affecting social behaviour
305 – Social groups.

This shows how a library uses the system to order books into sections which are easy to locate.

Another way to identify potential texts is to do a search on a library's information system to highlight books of interest, which may be available in other libraries. This is a computer-based system operated by typing in information on the text or book that you want. You can search using a number of criteria depending on the information you have. This includes:

◆ Author's name   ◆ Key word or topic.

◆ Title of the book

This enables you to a search with only a small amount of information.

Once you identify books that may be useful, you should be able to find them on the shelves. If they are not in stock, the books can then be requested; however, it can take over four weeks for a reserved book to become available. This is one reason why it is important to do this research work early in the project.

Besides textbooks, it is often worthwhile searching through journals for up-to-date research material or information on your research project. Town libraries tend not to keep academic journals, such as *Sociology Review*, but may keep popular journals such as *Nursing Times*. Good sources of academic journals are university libraries. You should be able to use the library as a casual user, or you could join as a member if you feel greater access to the books would be valuable. You usually have to pay an annual fee to become an external member of a university library.

ACTIVITY

Visit a library. Locate the following sections using the Dewey system.

◆   Family structure

◆   Research methods

◆   Business studies

◆   Topic of your own choice.

1   What is the Dewey number for each category?

2   What range of books are available?

3   How useful are the books shelved either side of your subject in relation to your topic?

Using academic libraries

Libraries at universities or colleges are likely to have a lot more up-to-date material. They are generally much larger than town libraries or libraries in schools or colleges. In university libraries, you can use a journal search system called ERIC. Here you type in your topic of interest or related words. It then gives a list of relevant articles which you can access. If you have access to a university library, it may be worth spending a day doing research and taking notes, if you are unable to take textbooks out.

Using CD-ROMs

You could do your search through CD-ROMs which catalogue academic journals, to enable you to discover which may be relevant to your topic. As this process is based on searching through key words, which might appear in the text, the results can be very broad. However, a summary of the text is given so researchers can decide if it is relevant to them. It also gives the journal date and page number. This reduces the time it would take to do a manual search through back-dated journals, as you can go directly to the edition and page required.

Again, it may be necessary to order copies of articles from other libraries and this will take time. So, this should be another of the activities carried out early in the research process.

How many books should be used in a literature search?

This depends on what is available. It is important that you 'read around' the topic area at the outset of the research, and this generally means reading more than one or two books.

It is also important to explore books that have a little information about your topic, as well as those that have a lot. Do not discard a text because it appears to have only a paragraph about your topic. This one paragraph may be of value and give you a worthwhile quote.

It is important that your bibliography has a sufficiently wide range of texts to indicate the extent of your reading.

Gleaning information

When carrying out the literature search, it is unlikely that you will want to, or have the time to, read every word in every book. You will need to use a range of skills to help you identify appropriate chapters and pages to read, and to ensure that you do not miss any essential sections. This can be achieved through techniques such as using the contents page or the index, skim reading or scanning.

Using the contents page

Most textbooks have a comprehensive contents page, which lists the titles of the chapters. This should be your first source of narrowing down what to read.

Look down the list of contents of a book on your subject to see if any chapters or words used might be relevant to your topic.

You may find a chapter that clearly relates to your topic area. On reading it, you may feel you need to extend your reading to other chapters in the textbook. Alternatively, it may be a self-contained piece of writing and all you need to cover in that particular book.

Using the index

You can also find what you need in a textbook by using the index. This is located at the back of the book.

NVQ 3 Care 11/7/01 2:38 PM Page iii

Contents

The contents page gives you some idea of what is in a book that is relevant to your needs

Index

abuse
  adults 119, 123–4, 125–6
  by care workers 124, 140
  carers 121, 123–4, 134
  children 118, 122–3, 125, 129–30, 138
  dealing with 132–3, 137–40
  definition 117
  disabled 124
  disclosures 131
  good practice 141
  inter agency teamwork 137–8
  legislation 122–4
  perpetrators 120–21, 135–6
  protection from 69, 137–8
  reporting 69, 124, 127–8, 133–4
  risk assessments 138–40
  self-inflicted 119, 121
  signs of 130–31
  stopping 126
  support for
    carers 134
    victims 134, 135–6
  by visitors 121
abusers 120–21, 135–6
Access to Medical Records Act 204–5
accidents
  distress caused by 94–5
  reporting 74–5, 94
addressing clients 55
advocacy, consent 230, 271
agencies see services and agencies
allergies
  anaesthetics 239, 272
  anaphylactic shock 239, 272
  clinical procedures 238, 239, 271, 272
  latex 239, 240, 272, 343
Alzheimer's disease 144, 209, 305
anaesthetics, allergy to 239, 272
anaphylactic shock 239, 272
Apollo Syndrome 186–7
appraisal 104–5
asthma 262, 289, 335
Attendance Allowance 318

bacteria 158–9
barium enemas 230
beds
  bridging 356–7

getting out of 355
naso-gastric feeding tubes 278
pressure sores 358–62
rolling over 356
behaviour, changes in 368
benefits
  carers 321–2
  child 318–19
  claim forms 323–5
  dental treatment 320
  disability 318, 321–2, 325
  entitlements 314, 317–18, 322
  eye tests 318
  fraudulent claims 324
  low income 309, 319–20
  payment methods 326–8
  pensions 317, 318
  prescriptions 318, 320
  residential home fees 318
  transport costs 318, 320
Benefits Agency 15, 317
biofeedback 393
bladder 380–81
bleeding 84–5
blindness see visual impairment
blood see body fluids and waste
blood pressure
  diastolic 259
  systolic 259
  taking 240, 250–9, 273, 286, 335
blood sampling
  blood sugar test 255–6, 284
  finger prick 255, 284
  frequent 255, 284
  phenylketonuria test 255, 281
  precautions 240, 273
  venipuncture 255, 281, 282–3
blood-borne viruses 162
  mucocutaneous exposure 163
  precautions 163 4, 240, 273
  transmission 163
body fluids and waste
  cleaning materials, disposal 170
  disposal 76, 170
  eye protection 164, 240, 273
  spillages 164, 170

  universal precautions 163–4, 240, 273
body mass index [BMI] 261, 262, 288, 289
body temperature 257, 285
bowel action 381–2
bronchitis 254, 281, 335
budgeting 309–10, 311
Burchescolposuspension 395
burns and scalds 91–2

Caldecott Guardians 30, 31, 34
Caldecott Principles 29–34
cardiac arrests 85–6, 92
care environments, definition 117
care planning meetings
  clients at 208, 208–9, 212, 213
  preparation 207
  proposals
    client agreement 214–16
    communicating 213 14
    imposition 215
    recording 212–13, 216
    stereotyping 209
care plans 235, 268
  abuse 127–8
  changing needs 219
    implementing 219–20
  mobility 357
  monitoring provision 217 19
  review processes 220–21
carers
  benefits 321–2
  effect of distress 378
  support for 330–31
case notes/files 235, 268
cash, security of 326, 328
catheters
  bags 400–1
  client procedures 333
  hygiene 249
  indwelling 249, 276–7, 400
  latex allergy 239, 272
  urine specimen collection 251–2
cerebral palsy 144, 151
Charters
  Benefits Agency 15
  Long-term Care 15
  Patients 15
Child Benefit [formerly Family Allowance] 318–19

The index gives you a more detailed idea of what is in a book and enables you to find it

Look through an index of a book on your subject for words which are relevant to your topic, and look up the relevant page numbers.

Remember, look up words which are closely related or which may be other ways of describing something. For example, if you are doing an investigation on children's games in the playground and how they have changed over time, you may look up words such as:

◆ *Games*

◆ *Activities*

◆ *Play*

◆ *Skipping*

◆ *Ball games*

◆ *Team games.*

All these headings may relate to different pieces of information about the same subject within one book.

An index is more detailed than the contents page as it identifies words or topics of interest within the text and refers to the page where they can be found. It is useful as it highlights minor references as well as major ones.

The disadvantage of the index is that it is compiled by the author of the book and therefore reflects what the author feels is important. This may not include the topic you are looking for, even if it is discussed in the book.

Nevertheless, using the index is still an efficient way of identifying whether a textbook contains information of interest to you.

Using the bibliography

Most textbooks have a bibliography at the end of each chapter or at the back of the book. The bibliography lists the books and articles that the author has used to support his or her writing. The books and articles are usually closely related to the topic and therefore a source of further reading. This can save you a lot of time searching for relevant material. The dates of publication are also given, so recent texts are easily identifiable. You can then use this information to carry out a library search to obtain the book.

Skim reading

This is a skill in which you cast your eye over a page very quickly, scanning it to pick out words of interest and relevance. If these words are identified, then the text can be read more carefully to see if it does cover the information required.

This is a quick technique, which allows a significant amount of material to be covered in a short time.

ACTIVITY

Skim read the section of text below using the skim reading technique. It is an excerpt of writing from page 14 of *Planning Play and the Early Years*, by P. Tassoni and K. Hucker.

   Identify the section which contains relevant information on industrialisation.

1   What is the main point being made about industrialisation?

2   Did you need to read every word in order to identify it?

3   How long did it take you to identify the appropriate section?

History of play

Various theorists have offered explanations to account for the origins, functions and pattern of play. Attitudes of society and images of childhood have influenced the care and activities provided for children through the ages.

   Until the 1800s, children were largely regarded as little adults. No special provision was made for them. Babies used to be swaddled in close-fitting blankets to prevent too much movement. Children also had to work from a young age. Once laws were established regarding child labour, the number of children per family went down as children then became a burden rather than an asset.

   Jean-Jacques Rousseau (1759), a French philosopher, was revolutionary in his call for children to be able to roam freely. Rousseau was probably the first thinker to identify the importance of play. He believed in free play and through his book *Emile* he outlined the need for the child to be allowed to explore freely in the early years of childhood, to discover for themselves without any constraints on them. He believed that to learn best, a child needed to be isolated. He suggested that play and work are all one for children until 10 or 12 years of age. However, despite his efforts, he was unable to convince eighteenth century society of the need for play.

   Play became more important in the late 1800s when industrialisation reduced the need for intensive labour and resulted in an increase in leisure time. Employment laws changed and restrictions were placed on young children working. This gave them more freedom than they had ever had before.

   Nevertheless, society still saw play and leisure as abnormal activities and work as a normal activity. To make play an acceptable activity, the Victorians focused on play with a purpose as it was felt that if people had free time, it should be used to improve themselves.

   Rousseau's work went on to influence other theorists such as Maria Montessori and Friedrich Froebel, although they tended to promote structured rather than free play.

Taking notes

Well-organised notes taken from the sources you have read will help you produce a good-quality investigation. Notes should include ideas and concepts as well as direct quotes.

   For quoting directly from sources, do not rely on your memory; the quotes should be part of your notes. Otherwise you will find that after reading several sources you will find it difficult to remember what you read or where you read it.

   Notes should be a succinct précis of the information. There should be enough detail to give the ideas and points of the author, but they should not be copied word for word. You could make a list of topics and texts that you could return to if you needed a quote.

One way of being organised when dealing with large amounts of material is to use a card index system. This is where you use a card for each text you use. Label the card with all the important details of the text. These are the title, author, date of edition, publisher and place. It is also worth noting where you got the book from and the Dewey number in case you want to find it again. This information also ensures that you have a full reference for anything you may wish to include in your write-up.

Use the card to note down important points from the book you are reading. If you are noting potential quotes, make sure you indicate that they are direct quotes by using speech marks. This will ensure you avoid plagiarism if you return to use the card at a later date. Direct quotations must be given in speech marks in any text you write, and accompanied by the author, date and page the quote comes from.

Acknowledging your sources

When writing research projects, many people use other writers' work and incorporate it into their work to support what they are doing. Sometimes other people's work is copied out word for word as a direct quote and sometimes writers put another author's ideas into their own words to support an idea they have themselves. This is fine as long as you make it clear that the quote or idea is not your own work.

Whenever other people's material is used in any piece of writing, it should be acknowledged – the author needs to say where the information came from. This is important because it is not acceptable to copy other people's work. Copying in this way is known as plagiarism.

If students copy an author's work without acknowledging the source, they may find their work fails.

To show clearly that information you have used is not your own, you need to know how to reference correctly.

Referencing

Good referencing is essential as it allows readers to check the source if they wish to.

There are a number of different ways to reference, but the Harvard system is most commonly used.

If you are writing other authors' ideas in your own words, you must acknowledge this by giving their name and the date of the publication in which you have read about their ideas – e.g. 'Smith (1999) suggested that …'.

If texts have been written by more than one person, the full author list should be mentioned the first time it is used, e.g. 'According to Smith, Brown and Jenkins (1993) …'. If the same book is used again, it can be referred to as Smith et al. (1993).

However, if you are directly quoting something that has appeared in another text, you must give author, date and page number. Directly quoted material usually appears indented in the text – e.g. Smith states:

… (1999, page 14)

The full details of the text should then appear in the bibliography. This allows readers to check the reference if they wish or to follow up by reading more by that particular author.

An alternative way of organising your records of secondary research might be to have cards based on topics rather than the texts themselves. This will enable you to identify potential quotes immediately when writing up aspects of the work. However, in the early stages of reading, it may be difficult to establish a list of headings which will work.

Therefore, a combination of the two methods would be useful. A card system is developed according to the texts, and a subject list is also developed. This will allow effective and efficient cross-referencing at the write-up stage.

Referencing and compiling the bibliography

There are conventions for compiling a bibliography which should be followed. The Harvard method is commonly used. It has the following headings:

Author	Date	Title	Publisher	Place where published
(Surname, initial)				

Generally, the title of the book is written in *italics* or **bold** or underlined to make it stand out. The date is the published date of the edition you have used and this should be in brackets. When using a number of books, these are recorded in the bibliography in alphabetical order according to the author.

Author	Date	Title	Publisher	Place
Apple, J	(1990)	*Sociology*	Lonlish	London
Davies, A	(1999)	*Women's roles*	Panguin	New York
Summers, G	(1997)	*Social lives*	Lonlish	London

If more than one person has written a textbook, then the referencing is slightly different, as in:

Tassoni, P and Hucker, K (2000) *Planning play and the early years*, Heinemann, Oxford.

In the body of your text, the book should be referred to as Tassoni and Hucker (2000).

If a text has been written by more than two authors, then the bibliography should list all the names of the authors, but if making reference to it in the text, you can write the name of the first author followed by et al. and the date (in brackets). Et al. means 'and the others' and is a form of shorthand to save you writing all the names out.

EXAMPLE

Davies, L, March, P and James, T (1987) *People talking*, Pienuin, London

The reference in the text would be Davies et al. (1987).

This is because long lists of authors' names will affect the flow of the text and make it more difficult for the reader to remember the reference.

Magazine articles and journals are referenced in a particular way as well. A magazine article is likely to be only part of the magazine, and therefore the exact pages must be indicated.

EXAMPLE

'Body survey', *Marie Claire*, No. 153, May 2001, pages 75–78

Being up to date

One issue to bear in mind when doing any kind of literature research, is the date of the material you are reading. It is important to remember that in some cases material goes out of date relatively quickly, so it is wise to try to research your topic using relatively recent books. Some material, however, does not go out of date due to its historical nature. The important thing is to be aware of your topic and the date of the publication and decide if this is an important correlation.

Unless a book is up to date you may not find the information you want in it

It is also important to remember that in some areas information and understanding is developing so fast that as soon as a piece of information is published, it is out of date.

Older texts can be useful as a way of generating ideas or hypotheses on which to base research. They can present a possibility of researching into issues at the time of publishing or to compare how things have changed. For example, if you were looking at how advice on parenting has changed, you might look at books written in the 1960s by parent experts of the day, such as Dr Benjamin Spock, and compare the ideas with those of more modern-day parenting authors, such as Miriam Stoppard.

As you may not have access to specialist journals or higher-level student work, such as a thesis, it is unlikely that you will have access to the cutting-edge information on a subject. However, this is an area where the media can help. The media often pick up stories of new developments or ideas, and so it is worth while being aware of this.

Being critical about books

All authors have a point of view about the topics they write on. It is important that you are aware of this as you read the texts, so that you are alert to and become aware of any possible slant on the text. Bias on the part of the author will obviously affect the way material is presented.

Bias may be evident through the language that is used. For example, an article written by a baby milk company which does not present a balanced view on breast versus bottle feeding could be said to be biased in favour of the company and the product it makes.

ACTIVITY

Can you give other examples of where bias may occur?

Bias may be obvious in that the author clearly states that the views are his or her own. It may be that the text is written by a female author, who has strong feelings about the role of women in society. Therefore, her views and perceptions are likely to come through in her writing.

Another way in which bias may be detected is through criticism of a researcher's work by other researchers. This will highlight areas where you may need to be careful when using the findings. Bias in any text does not necessarily mean that the work is invalid and shouldn't be used. The important point is that you are aware of the bias and reflect that in the way you use the material. Bias, however, can be very difficult to detect so it won't always be easy. Make sure you are aware of any clues which might help you, such as the authors' interests or the way they have conducted their research.

What to do when there is limited published material

Sometimes there is very limited published material on the topic you are studying. You may have tried a detailed literature research and come up with very little. This may mean either

◆ that the topic is very current,

or

◆ that it hasn't been researched very much.

If the topic is current, the main source of information may be the newspapers or the Internet, as these tend to carry more up-to-date information. CD-ROMs of recently published newspapers may also be a useful source of information. These may also be useful sources for topics which haven't been researched much, but this may also be due to the fact that the topic is not an easy one to study. In both cases, there will be a broader scope for first-hand research. It will, however, be more difficult to analyse the findings as there will be little to compare them with.

Using documents as a source of information

The definition of 'document' is any material that provides you with information for your research, not including books, media sources or statistics. It may include:

◆ reports

◆ memos

◆ publicity material from organisations

◆ minutes of meetings or records from organisations.

There are often key reports on topics which you may wish to use if they are relevant to your work.

An example of a key report would be the report into eating habits of the UK population in the early 1980s by the National Advisory Committee on Nutrition Education (NACNE). This gave the foundation for the healthy eating campaigns which were an important part of health education in the late 1980s and 1990s. Another key report in health care was the *Health of the Nation* report which looked at the causes of wider health problems such as cancers and heart disease in the population. These would be essential background reading if you were looking at healthy eating or diet-related disorders.

Reports

Currently, a key document in the Care Sector is the *Fit for the Future* report, published by the Department of Health, setting out the standards which all care homes must follow in the new millennium. Any student who is investigating care of the elderly should look at this report as part of their research.

When using a report, it is important to consider who was involved in writing it and what their brief was. It may also be useful to look for any other commentary that there may be on the report, as it may help you to set the report in context. Often report committees are made up of people from a wide range of backgrounds in order to get a broad set of views, so that it is relevant to a broad range of the population. Such reports should not be taken as being completely accurate, as they are one view of a situation, but they will provide food for thought.

Fit For The Future?
National Required Standards
for Residential and Nursing
Homes for Older People

Consultation Document

Modernising Social Services

The Health Education Council

A discussion paper on
**proposals for nutritional guidelines for
health education in Britain**

NACNE September 1983

Reprinted March 1984

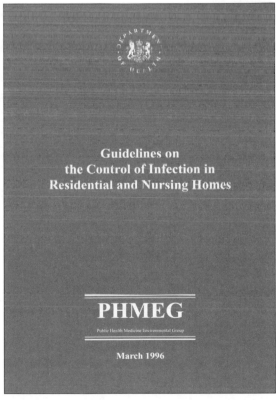

Guidelines on
the Control of Infection in
Residential and Nursing Homes

PHMEG

Public Health Medicine Environmental Group

March 1996

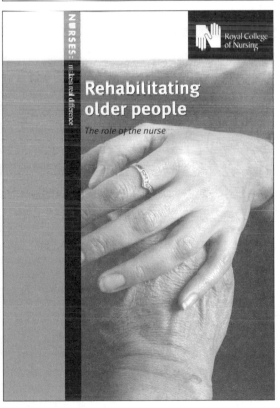

Royal College
of Nursing

NURSES: making a real difference

**Rehabilitating
older people**

The role of the nurse

Documents such as these are valuable sources of information

Useful reports for health and social care students

There is a wealth of reports related to health and social care which provide valuable secondary research for a wide range of investigations or projects. A number of examples are given in the table below.

Table 3.1   Reports on health and social care

Name of report and date	Information covered	Published by
Fit for the Future 1999	The guidelines and standards which all care establishments for the elderly need to work towards.	Department of Health The Stationery Office
Health of the Nation 1990	A report which summarised the five main areas of health: ◆ cancer ◆ sexual health ◆ coronary heart disease ◆ accidents ◆ mental health. It made recommendations for changes to improve health.	The Stationery Office
Drug Use, Smoking and Drinking among Teenagers in 1999	A survey monitoring the use of alcohol, drugs and tobacco among young people.	Department of Health, Home Office and the UK Anti-Drugs Co-ordination Unit The Stationery Office, London
British Social Attitudes 2000	A survey of contemporary attitudes.	British Society of Gerontology
Children's Act 1989	A report on changes to children's rights and the responsibilities of people working with them.	Department of Health The Stationery Office
Changing Times: Work and Leisure in Post-Industrial Society 2000	A survey into work and leisure patterns in modern society.	Oxford University Press
Social Trends	Annual report giving a comprehensive guide to statistics on a range of social issues, including population, health, education and housing.	Office for National Statistics
Health Statistics Quarterly	Quarterly publication on health	Office for National Statistics
Human Development Report 2000	Annual report on the disparities between the richest and poorest nations.	United Nations

Reports are constantly being published so it is important to keep up to date. Extracts from new surveys and reports are often reported in the media, either in the newspapers or on television. These media sources of information can alert you to new reports which you can then research in more detail.

Minutes as part of 'documents'

Minutes are the official records of meetings. Most minutes are open documents which you may be able to analyse if you felt it was relevant. For example, all pre-school providers who wish to access government funding now have to be inspected by OfSTED. If you were looking at the effect OfSTED has had on playgroups, the minutes of a local playgroup committee meeting may be a good way to assess how OfSTED is influencing discussion and action at committee level.

Minutes of meetings are documents that can be researched to discover what was discussed and decided

When using minutes, it is important to remember that they are a summary of what happened in the meeting and not a word-for-word account. Therefore, their use can be limited. Also, they are only one person's view of what happened and what was said. It is also likely that any confidential discussion that takes place will not be published as part of the main minutes, if at all.

Minutes may also be intended for internal use only, so it is important that issues of confidentiality and privacy are considered if you are using minutes as a source of information in your work.

The value of minutes will depend on your enquiry. If you are looking at a local issue, it may be worth looking at the minutes of the local council meetings as this may give you information on the views and ideas of the local people.

Memos when used as part of 'documents'

These are internal correspondence within organisations that can give you an insight into how an organisation is operating. Copies are often kept. Memos may give you important information about issues of the moment. Often, current affairs programmes or newspapers carry stories about 'leaked memos' which give an insight into how someone may be thinking about or dealing with an issue.

Using promotional material

Many organisations produce promotional material. This includes publicity information from various organisations, brochures or prospectuses from schools and colleges, product information, information from political parties or local groups.

This information can be used in research projects as a source of information. This material is likely to be biased as it will have been written with a particular purpose in mind. Nevertheless, it can be useful, if only to confirm your conclusions about an issue.

Using promotional material as primary research

Promotional material can also be used as a primary research method. The material can be analysed in a number of different ways, depending on the focus of the study. Promotional material could be analysed for gender or race issues, method of presentation, use of language, and so on. Using promotional material as a primary research method is covered in Chapter 9.

Research using the Internet

The Internet is a massive network of computerised information, possibly the greatest store of information ever to be found through a single medium. It is therefore a great way to try to find out information about any project you are doing. For any researcher with access to a computer and the Internet, all this information is literally at your fingertips. However, because there is so much information, you may find yourself spending a lot of time 'surfing' or browsing through sites trying to find what you want. This section will give you a few tips on using the Internet efficiently.

Getting started

To be able to find information on the Internet, you need to have a piece of software called a web browser. This allows you to look at the pages of the World Wide Web.

Web addresses

All sites on the Internet have web addresses. It starts with http://www. This is a form of coding which is known as URLs (Uniform Resource Locators). It works just like an address on a letter; that is, it tells the computer where to find a website. If you know the address where to find the information you are looking for, you can find it by typing the address into the location section at the top of the Internet screen, then press return or go and wait for the site to be downloaded.

A website address

You will find that many websites have similar endings or suffixes. This tells you something about the type of site it is. Common endings are as follows:

.ac	academic body or institution
.co	business
.com	commercial organisation
.gov	government body or office
.net	Internet provider
.org	organisation.

Suffixes can also indicate what country a site is located in. For example, British-based websites are .uk; French websites are .fr. An example is the Department for Education site, which is www.dfee.gov.uk; a college would be www.anycollege.ac.uk; and so on.

Searching for information

If you do not know the site addresses for the information you are looking for, you will need to carry out a search. A search engine is a website that can be used to find other websites. You simply type in a key word and the search engine will search the Internet for relevant sites.

Sometimes this will produce a vast number of sites, far more that you need. Many of these may be irrelevant, as the search will identify any site with the words you have listed. One way to avoid this is to use speech marks, " ", or the + sign, so that

A search engine

the Internet will find only sites where the phrase appears together. For example, if in searching for MMR immunisation you present it a "MMR vaccination" or MMR+vaccination, the information found should be more specific and focused.

Advanced searches

Some search engines allow you to do more advanced searches and use words such as 'and', 'or' and 'not'. This allows you to be far more specific in your search. For example, if researching into adolescent diabetes, you could focus the search as "diabetes and (adolescents and not elderly)". You can also use the word 'near' on some advanced searches and this will find sites where the keywords are no more than 10 words apart.

One of the most powerful search engines for this type of advanced search is Altavista (http://www.altavista.com).

Search sites

There are numerous search sites which you may like to use when searching for information. Some of the popular ones are listed below.

Altavista	http://www.altavista.com
Yahoo!	http://www.yahoo.com
Excite	http://www.excite.com
Webcrawler	http://www.webcrawler.com
Lycos	http://www.lycos.com

All search engines work in different ways and can find different information. Therefore, is it useful if you search using a number of engines rather than just one.

Going back to find information

When you find a site which is useful, you can print out the information. This will also give you the website address if you want to go back to it again in the future. If you just jot down notes from the site, take the full address of the site to make sure that you can find it again when you need to.

Another way of ensuring you find information again is to add useful sites to your Bookmark or Favourites menu. This is an icon on the tool bar of your Internet page. It allows you to store a favourite site so you can return to it at the click of a button.

Useful sites for health and social care students

As we have already said, there are numerous sites which contain useful information on health and social care. There are too many to name them all, but below are a few of the popular sites which may prove to be a useful starting point for a research project.

Table 3.2   Popular websites for health and social care information

Site	Address	Information provided
Health World	http://www.healthy.net	Large health site with information on all aspects of health
NursingNet	http://www.nursingnet.com	Source of nursing resources
Reuters Health	http://www.reutershealth.com	Health news, reviews and opinions
Department for Education	http://www.dfee.gov.uk	Source of information on education in the UK today
British Political Parties	http://www.labour.org.uk http://www.libdems.org.uk http://www.conservative-party.org.uk	Information on the policies of the three main political parties in the UK
The NHS	http://www.nhs.uk	Information on the NHS, including a potted history of health issues in post-war Britain (www.nhs50.nhs.uk)
British Heart Foundation	http://www.bhf.org.uk	Lots of information on heart disease and how it can be prevented
Encyclopedia Britannica	http://www.eb.com	A very comprehensive source of reference on many issues

Because of its wealth of information, the Internet is worth using as one of your sources of secondary research, along with traditional textbooks. Most libraries now have computer facilities with Internet access for library users.

ACTIVITY

Test your knowledge of literature searches by doing this multiple-choice test.

1 The Harvard system is set out as:
   a Surname, year of publication, title, place of publication.
   b Title (underlined), surname, place of publication, year of publication.
   c Title, year of publication, place of publication, surname.
   d Surname, title, year of publication, place of publication.

2 A bibliography is:
   a All the books in the library relevant to the topic.
   b Any source material which the author could have used on the topic.
   c A list of the sources the author used for the work.
   d A reference to the exact sections of source books which have been used.

3 The Dewey system is:
   a A form of search engine.
   b A three-digit book classification system.
   c A way to carry out research.
   d A method for reading around a subject.

4 A search engine is:
   a An Internet explorer.
   b A website which looks for information.
   c An Internet provider which gives information.
   d A special type of CD-ROM which has information on it.

5 Plagiarism is:
   a Quoting other people's work.
   b Using other people's work as a way of supporting your own findings.
   c Using too many secondary sources.
   d Copying other people's work without acknowledging it.

6 'Tassoni and Hucker (2000) suggested that............' is a form of:
   a Bibliography.   c Direct quoting.
   b Referencing.   d Plagiarism.

7 A literature base is:
   a A systematic collection of material relevant to your topic.
   b A place where books are kept.
   c Part of the library where searches can be carried out.
   d A list of all the information you have collected.

Answers to test:					
1	a	4	b	7	a
2	c	5	d		
3	b	6	b		

Further reading

Bell, J (1999) *Doing your research project*, Open University Press, Buckingham
Green, S (2000) *Research methods*, Stanley Thornes, Cheltenham
Tassoni, P and Hucker, K (2000) *Planning play and the early years*, Heinemann, Oxford

4 Using statistics

Statistics produced by others can provide very useful material for any research project. In this chapter we will explore the role of statistics in research and look at the possible sources of statistics relevant to the health care area. This chapter covers:

◆ Why do we have statistics?

◆ Who collects and uses statistical information?

◆ Official and unofficial statistics

◆ Bias

◆ The main sources of statistics

◆ The uses of national statistics

◆ Ensuring validity and reliability.

Why do we have statistics?

In the health and social care area we are lucky because there are a lot of very useful statistics which are collected centrally by the government. Using statistics can be one way of looking at what has happened in the past and allowing comparison with current trends. Statistics can show what has happened across a number of years.

Statistics can also be used to give an insight into the topic being researched or to provide a basis on which to develop an idea. For example, someone investigating if there are enough services to meet the needs of single-parent families, may look at statistics which show the changes in the percentage of lone-parent families as a source of background information on the topic.

Data that has already been collected can also be used to test hypotheses instead of carrying out original research in the field. Primary research can be expensive and therefore an investigation drawing entirely on statistics produced by others may be the only way the research can be afforded. Statistics can be analysed and used to study trends over time. It may also be possible to make comparisons between different groups. This information cannot generally be obtained through primary research methods. One example of this is life expectancy figures. These have been collected throughout the last century by the government and therefore provide detailed information on how life expectancy has changed.

ACTIVITY

The statistics for households by type of household and family in Great Britain between 1961 and 1998–99 are given below.

Households: by type of household and family (Great Britain)

	1961	1971	1981	1991	Percentages 1998–99
One person					
Under pensionable age	4	6	8	11	14
Over pensionable age	7	12	14	16	15
Two or more unrelated adults	5	4	5	3	2
One-family households					
Couple					
No children	26	27	26	28	30
1–2 dependent children	30	26	25	20	19
3 or more dependent children	8	9	6	5	4
Non-dependent children only	10	8	8	8	6
Lone parent					
Dependent children	2	3	5	6	7
Non-dependent children only	4	4	4	4	3
Multi-family households	3	1	1	1	1
All households					
(=100%)(millions)	16.3	17.5	22.4	22.4	21.4

Source: *Social Trends 2000*

1   What information might be drawn from the figures as background to a piece of work on services and support available for single-parent families?

2   What other trends are shown through the data?

3   How might this be used to give ideas for areas of research?

ACTIVITY

Study the life expectancy figures given below.

Expectation of life at selected ages: by gender
United Kingdom   Years

	1911	1931	1951	1971	1991	1997	2011	2021
Males								
At birth	50.4	58.0	66.1	68.8	73.2	74.6	77.4	78.6
At age								
20	44.0	46.5	49.4	50.9	54.2	55.5	58.0	59.1
40	27.5	29.5	30.8	31.8	35.2	36.4	39.0	40.0
60	13.7	14.5	14.8	15.3	17.7	18.8	21.0	22.0
80	4.9	4.8	5.0	5.5	6.4	6.7	7.7	8.3
Females								
At birth	53.9	62.0	70.9	75.0	78.8	79.6	81.6	82.7
At age								
20	46.4	49.4	53.6	56.7	59.6	60.3	62.0	63.1
40	29.8	32.2	34.9	37.3	40.0	40.8	42.5	43.5
60	15.3	16.4	17.8	19.8	21.9	22.6	24.1	25.1
80	5.6	5.6	5.9	6.9	8.4	8.5	9.1	9.9

Source: *Social Trends 2000*

1   What are the trends that the data is showing?

2   Why do you think the data is classified by gender?

3   How might you account for the trends identified?

4   What further information might you like to have if you were doing further research on this topic?

However, most research is carried out for a particular purpose and may not specifically meet the focus of the work.

Over the century, society has become more centrally organised and this has increased the need for written records, including the need for statistical information on individuals, clients and customers, for example. For every individual, records on them begin with the birth certificate which parents receive once they register the birth of a child. Parents are required to do this by law.

CERTIFIED COPY **OF AN ENTRY**
Pursuant to the Births and   Deaths Registration Act 1953

DAF 218901

BIRTH		**Entry No.**

Registration district	Administrative area
Sub-district	

1.	Date and place of birth	CHILD	

2. Name and surname		3. Sex

4. Name and surname	FATHER	

5. Place of birth	6. Occupation

7. Name and surname	MOTHER

8.(a) Place of birth	8.(b) Occupation

9.(a) Maiden surname	9.(b) Surname at marriage if different from maiden surname

10. Usual address (if different from place of child's birth)

11. Name and surname (if not the mother or father) INFORMANT	12. Qualification

13. Usual address
(if different from
that in 10 above)

14. I certify that the particulars entered above are true to the best of my knowledge and belief	Signature of informant

15. Date of registration	16. Signature of registrar

17. Name given
after registration,
and surname

SPECIMEN

Certified to be a true copy of an entry in a register in my custody.

.... { *Superintendent Registrar   Date
                                                                 *Registrar

*Strike out whichever does not apply

CAUTION: THERE ARE OFFENCES RELATING TO FALSIFYING OR ALTERING A CERTIFICATE AND USING
OR POSSESSING A FALSE CERTIFICATE. ©CROWN COPYRIGHT

WARNING: A CERTIFICATE IS NOT EVIDENCE OF IDENTITY.

A birth certificate is one way information is recorded about people

This has a range of information on it, which ensures that an individual is 'logged' into the social welfare system. Following this, a baby is usually registered with a doctor and so a file of notes begins to be built up on their health record. This also ensures that the baby is in the automatic system for access to immunisations and health checks.

Every time you fill out a form, information about you is being stored somewhere.

Make a list of all the times when individuals may be required to fill out forms.

Think about how the information may be used in each case.

Who collects and uses statistical information?

All types of organisations collect information. They may be private businesses, statutory bodies or voluntary organisations.

A private business is an organisation that carries out its activities for profit. Statutory bodies are organisations that are linked to the government and often provide services which are funded by the state. Voluntary organisations are organisations that provide particular services which may not be available through the state system.

Table 4.1 Organisations that collect information

Type of organisation	Examples	What information they may collect	Why they collect it
Private businesses	Banks, building societies, shops and supermarkets.	Information about their customers' income and outgoings, behaviour patterns, such as saving and spending patterns.	So they can provide appropriate services for their customers. They can make sure they meet their needs and keep them happy. It also provides information for marketing purposes.
Statutory bodies	Central government, local authorities, councils, educational establishments, health care providers, CSA.	Information required may vary according to the aim of the organisation. For example, to plan the number of primary school places needed over a number of years, the local education authority needs birth rates in order to make sure there are enough places.	In some cases, the information may be used for planning services such as education, health care or housing provision.
Voluntary bodies	Shelter, Age Concern, Help the Aged, Imperial Cancer Research.	Information may be collected on the numbers of people they are helping or providing support for. They may also collect information on their individual needs and living experiences.	Voluntary organisations often act as pressure groups to try to improve things for the individuals they represent. They may use the information to support issues they wish to promote.

EXAMPLE

Gathering statistical information: loyalty cards

Most supermarkets now have loyalty cards, which they promote as a way that customers can save money. The development of loyalty cards allowed the supermarkets to acquire a lot of detailed information about their customers. This included income as well as shopping habits.

When customers use their store card at the checkout this also allows the shop to collect information on the products people prefer to buy. They are able to identify the various products and brands consumers buy. This enables them to provide the choice of products to meet the needs and wants of their individual customers. It also enables them to provide special offers to maximise spending in their stores. It also gives the organisation a bank of statistical material, which they can sell to other organisations. For example, a food manufacturer may wish to buy information to help them design a new product or develop the marketing of an old product.

This example shows why organisations may choose to collect statistics and how they use them for their own benefit.

Official and unofficial statistics

Many organisations that collect statistics for public use are official bodies or semi-official bodies. Many are linked to the government either at central or local level, or they are organisations financed by the government, such as the Sports Council or the Equal Opportunities Commission.

There is no clear boundary between official and unofficial statistics, but the source of the statistics does affect what statistics are collected, how they are collected and the way they are interpreted. It may also influence whether they are made available to the general public.

It is important to realise at the start that there are many different reasons for collecting statistics.

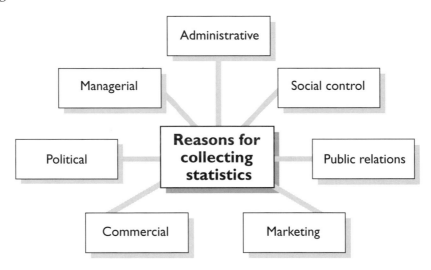

There are various reasons why statistical data is collected

This shows that plenty of information is collected which can be applied to a number of different purposes.

It may be possible to find statistics on almost any topic you want to research. They will always provide a good starting point and a way of generating ideas.

The reason behind the collecting of the statistics will affect the focus or slant which can be put on the process, from the collecting of the data to its analysis. This can introduce bias.

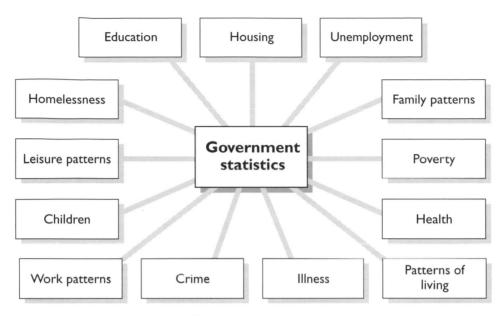

The government gathers statistics on a wide range of matters

Bias

Given that statistics are collected for a specific reason, you have to be aware that the statistics you are dealing with will have been collected with a specific focus in mind. This is known as bias, which means an underlying slant on something that may not be obvious from the questions asked. Researchers may hold particular views on a topic and these can influence the way data is collected (see Chapter 7).

Bias, whether intentional or unintentional, will affect the results obtained. Researchers can also manipulate results to give a particular emphasis.

Information collected by different groups can still be used as long as you are aware of the bias when you use it. Researchers may wish to look back at the sources of such research in order to help them understand the way the data may have been manipulated.

Statistics will therefore need to be interpreted with care and used with data from other sources to support it.

It may be that you are specifically interested in the way the bias is presented as this may give you information for your work.

Generally, the statistics kept by government agencies are the most reliable and useful forms of statistics. They contain a wealth of information, some of which can be related to all aspects of the health and care field.

The main sources of statistics

National and local government offices produce many statistics. Often these are used to help plan service provision across the country. This official data is collected very carefully and analysed in depth to ensure that the findings are as accurate as possible. The procedures used have helped to form what is considered to be good practice in data collection.

One of the biggest data collection exercises is the census which takes place every ten years. The latest one was on 29 April 2001. An extract from the census form is shown below.

How to complete the remaining questions

Remember to use black or blue ink.

Put a tick in the appropriate box, like this ✔. *If you mark the wrong box, fill in the box and put a tick in the right one, like this* ■
✔

Where you are required to write in an answer please use CAPITAL LETTERS and leave one space between each word. Start a new line if a word will not fit.

7 **What is your country of birth**

✔ **Elsewhere,** *please write in the present name of the country*

| S | O | U | T | H | | | |
| A | F | R | I | C | A | | |

Household Accommodation

H1 **What type of accommodation does your household occupy?**

A *whole* **house or bungalow that is:**

☐ Detached

✔ Semi-detached

☐ Terraced (including end-terrace)

A flat, maisonette, or apartment that is:

☐ In a purpose-built block of flats or tenement

☐ Part of a converted or shared house (includes bed-sits)

☐ In a commercial building (for example, in an office building, or hotel, or over a shop)

H4 **Do you have a bath/shower *and* toilet for use only by your household?**

✔ Yes

☐ No

H5 **What is the lowest floor level of your household's living accommodation?**

☐ Basement or semi-basement

✔ Ground floor (street level)

■ First floor (floor above street level)

☐ Second floor

☐ Third or fourth floor

☐ Fifth floor or higher

H8 **Does your household own or rent the accommodation?**

◆ ✔ *one box only.*

☐ Owns outright
➤ Go to **H10**

✔ Owns with a mortgage or loan
➤ Go to **H10**

☐ Pays part rent and part mortgate (shared ownership)
➤ Go to **H10**

☐ Rents
➤ Go to **H9**

☐ Lives here rent free
➤ Go to **H9**

H9 **Who is your landlord?**

☐ Council (Local Authority)

☐ Housing Association
Housing Co-operative
Charitable Trust
Registered Social Landlord

☐ Private landlord or letting agency

☐ Employer of a household member

☐ Relative or friend of a household member

☐ Other

H10 Please turn the page.

count me in
Census2001

This is your Census!
Put yourself in the picture

The Census is a count of the whole UK population that only takes place every 10 years. Census information will be used to share out billions of pounds of public money in years to come. To make sure everyone benefits, we need the whole picture.

1 We all need the Census

Census information is used to benefit us all – we all need to be included so we can get the services we need in the future.

2 Your information is confidential

Census forms are held in the strictest confidence – and are not released for 100 years!

3 We all need to be included

The Census is the only complete picture of the nation we have – it is impossible to plan services for invisible people.

4 The only way to see the full picture

The Census is a unique set of facts and figures because it counts everyone in the country at the same time – there is no other way of capturing a complete picture of the nation.

5 Post it back

Simply fill in the Census form on 29 April and post it back in the reply-paid envelope.

national STATISTICS

Remember
29 April is Census Day

A summary of the major official sources of statistics is given in Table 4.2. You can find this information in local libraries or you can purchase relevant publications from Her Majesty's Stationery Office (HMSO). You can also search for information on the Internet.

Table 4.2   Government publications of statistics

Title	Frequency of publication	
Social Trends	Annual	This publication covers a range of topics showing the trends over recent years. It includes population changes, family structure, employment patterns, housing, poverty and wealth. It also covers changes over time and is therefore a good source of information for discussion.
Regional Trends	Annual	Similar to Social Trends but covers information about a region rather than national.
The General Household Survey	Annual	A large-scale survey, which is carried out between censuses and provides information on populations and households.
Census	Every 10 years. The last census was carried out in 2001. Information will take several years to be published.	Every household in the country is required by law to fill out the 10-year census. It is a national piece of research and therefore provides data across England, Northern Ireland, Scotland and Wales. It is concerned with factual data such as household size and composition, employment and ownership of 'white goods'. White goods include items such as washing machines, fridges and freezers. It allows comparison across the regions.
New Earnings Survey	Annual	Started in 1970, this is based on a survey of 1% of employees. Each year the same employees are tracked, using their National Insurance number, and information about their earnings is recorded.
Labour Force Survey	Quarterly	A survey of 60,000 households which provides information on earnings and the type of households in which people live. It provides a way of linking earnings to social environment. It includes forms of earners, but the sample is relatively small.
Family Expenditure Survey	Annual	This survey draws on a sample of 6,600 households across the UK. It collects data, over a period of two weeks, on all aspects of family income and how it is spent. It records information on spending on housing, food, clothes, fuel and power, alcohol, tobacco, and so on.

ACTIVITY

Study the data produced by the *Family Expenditure Survey*.

Household expenditure: by income grouping, 1997–98

United Kingdom

	Quintile groups of households					Percentages
	Bottom fifth	Next fifth	Middle fifth	Next fifth	Top fifth	All households
Food	23	20	19	16	14	17
Leisure goods and services	13	15	16	17	20	17
Motoring and fares	11	15	16	19	18	17
Housing	16	16	15	15	16	16
Household goods and services	13	13	14	13	14	13
Clothing and footwear	6	5	5	6	6	6
Fuel, light and power	6	5	4	3	3	4
Alcohol	4	4	4	5	4	4
Tobacco	3	3	2	2	1	2
Other goods and services	4	4	5	4	4	4
All household expenditure (=100%)(£ per week)	171	218	305	407	556	331

Source: *Family Expenditure Survey*

1   How useful is this information in providing an insight into spending patterns across Britain?

2   How does the pattern of spending in an average household reflect modern lifestyles?

   Consider:
   ◆   Work patterns
   ◆   Leisure activities/social life
   ◆   Transportation.

3   How might you expect this to differ if you were comparing it to household spending in the 1950s?

The majority of official statistics are presented in a clear, understandable format, often in tables or graphs. This makes them easy to use, as long as you have studied the information which is provided.

An example of a table from *Social Trends* is given below.

Fertility rates: by age of mother at childbirth

United Kingdom Live births per 1,000 women

	1961	1971	1981	1991	1997	1998
Under 20	37	50	28	33	30	31
20–24	173	154	107	89	75	74
25–29	178	155	130	120	105	102
30–34	106	79	70	87	89	90
35–39	51	34	22	32	39	40
40 and over	16	9	5	5	7	8
All ages	91	84	62	64	60	59

Source: Office for National Statistics; General Register Office for Scotland; Northern Ireland Statistics and Research Agency

Graphs are another popular way for official statistics to be presented. Line graphs are often used to show patterns of change over a number of years. They are also a useful way to show comparative trends. For example, the graph below shows changes in places for residential care of the elderly since 1981. It clearly shows how there has been an increase in the number of places in private homes compared to a decrease in places in local authority provision.

Places in residential care homes for elderly people: by type of care home

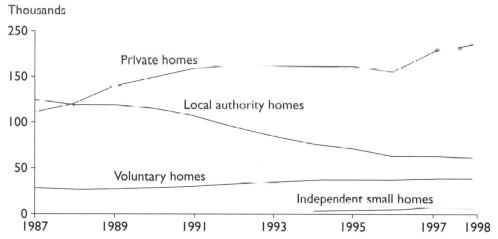

Source: Department of Health; National Assembly for Wales; Department of Health and Social Services, Northern Ireland

---

ACTIVITY

How might you use this type of graph in an investigation into care of the elderly?

Pie charts and bar charts are other methods used to present statistics. Two examples are given below.

Social security benefit expenditure: by recipient group, 1998–99

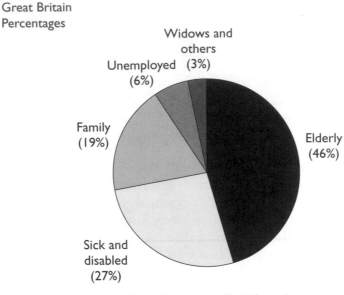

Great Britain
Percentages

(Source: Department of Social Security)

Pie chart

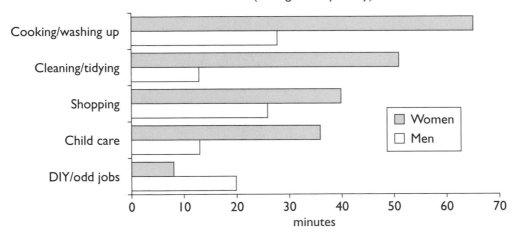

Domestic chores: unpaid work in the UK
(average time per day)

(Source: Office for National Statistics, Oct. 2000)

Bar chart

Much of this statistical information is readily available in local libraries. A librarian will be able to direct you towards the sources of statistics relevant to your work. However, sometimes these materials have to be used in the library; they cannot be borrowed because they are expensive and libraries have only one copy. However, most government-generated documents and statistics can be bought from Her Majesty's Stationery Office.

Office for National Statistics

The Office for National Statistics (ONS) is the government agency responsible for compiling, analysing and disseminating social, economic and demographic statistics for the United Kingdom. It is also responsible for the census and health statistics.

The ONS is a useful starting point if you want any data on these areas. They are generally up to date and also have statistics going back a number of years, which are useful for analysing trends over time.

They can be contacted through the National Statistics Public Enquiry Service or via their website (www.ons.gov.uk)

The uses of national statistics

Statistics can be used in a number of different ways:

◆ They are a useful way to look at trends over time. This must always be carried out with caution, as it is easy to attribute changes inappropriately. As the information is based on the past, it is difficult to go back and test such conclusions. Sometimes changes can be coincidental or linked to something which hasn't yet been identified.

◆ Statistics can also be used to look at what has stayed the same for a number of years. It can be just as important to notice that there hasn't been a significant change. For example, the fact that average life expectancy rates have not increased for people in the lower groups of the Registrar-General Social Class List, despite improvements in housing, health care and the provision of social welfare.

ACTIVITY

Study the data on adults living with their parents below.

Adults living with their parents: by gender and age

England			Percentages
	1977–78	1991	1998–99
Males			
20–24	52	50	56
25–29	19	19	24
30–34	9	9	11
Females			
20–24	31	32	38
25–29	9	9	11
30–34	3	5	4

Source: *National Dwellings and Household Survey* and *Survey of English Housing*, Department of the Environment.

> 1   What are the general trends in the data shown between
> ◆ 1977–78 and 1991
>
> ◆ 1991 and 1998–99?
>
> 2   Can you suggest any reasons for the trends shown?
>
> 3   How might you use this information to support a research project?

◆ Statistics can provide background information to support an area of study. Providing some national or historical figures may help to 'set the scene' or the context in which the work is placed. It may provide supporting information to show why a specific focus has been taken. For example, a piece of work on 'adolescent girls' smoking habits' may be supported by studying the trends in smoking patterns of the under-18s in general.

◆ Statistics can be used to compare and contrast official findings with your own research findings. If you are researching adolescent girls' smoking habits you may wish to compare the results of smoking patterns against the national statistics to see how closely your findings replicate the national picture.

◆ Statistics can also be used to compare information between groups – for example, you may wish to compare patterns of adolescent smoking between adolescents in different social classes.

◆ Statistics can provide data which is otherwise difficult to obtain or replicate, either because it is not easily accessible to you or because it covers information from the past. This may include information on patterns of homelessness or death and birth rates.

There is so much information available in the form of statistics and it is easy to collect too much and be overwhelmed with the amount of information. Students often make the mistake of putting too much into their research projects and sometimes gather information that is irrelevant to the topic being covered. It is important to be very strict when selecting statistics to include, and to make sure not to include material which does not illuminate or add anything to the work.

Ensuring validity and reliability

It is essential that any statistics used should be assessed for their validity and reliability.

Reliability

Data is considered to be reliable if the findings can be repeated by someone else. Reliable data means that if a different researcher carried out the same piece of research at a different time, the results would be similar or at least in line with what was previously found. This also assumes that whatever has been measured is the same and that the attitudes of those doing the measuring weren't different. For example, two pieces of research into the percentage of income spent on housing, by different researchers within a short time span, should throw up similar findings.

Findings are likely to be different, however, if the time span between the pieces of research is longer – for example, you could reasonably expect a change in the percentage income spent on housing if two studies were completed five years apart.

Validity

Validity is a more complicated term. For data to be considered valid, the method used to collect the data and the focus of the research must be relevant to the conclusion drawn. The question to be asked is 'Does the research method actually measure what it claims it is supposed to be measuring?' Researchers can sometimes draw indirect conclusions from a piece of research, but unless the research specifically looked at that factor, the findings may misinterpret the real situation and therefore not be valid.

If a piece of research is not reliable then it is unlikely to be valid. However, reliable data can at the same time be not valid as it may not measure what it sets out to do, although the results may be repeatable.

Representativeness

Another factor which can affect the quality of any data is the extent to which it represents the sections of the population it aims to cover.

It can be easy to apply conclusions to the whole of a section of the population based on data gained from a very small sample of people which is not representative of the whole. It is therefore important that the sample chosen for any research is carefully thought out.

For example, if you are researching the social life of elderly people in care homes, then the sample must be from that group and not just any elderly person regardless of where he or she lives. Conclusions based on a sample of 70% of elderly people who live in care homes and 30% who live in their own home would not be representative of that population, and therefore any findings attributed to social life in care homes would not be valid or reliable.

More information on sampling can be found in Chapters 6 and 7.

Generally, official statistics produced by the Office for Population, Census and Survey will be based on a carefully chosen sample.

Difficulties may arise if a response rate is low, as often happens with questionnaires. Data based on low response rates can skew the findings as respondents may be more heavily weighted from one social group than another.

Summary

Statistics are very useful in research. They can be used to provide background information about the area being studied or to support any findings that may arise out of primary research. However, approach statistics with caution. Do not take them at face value. Make sure they are valid, reliable and representative, and therefore relevant to the work. Choose reputable sources for statistics as these are more likely to be objective and to have been carried out correctly.

ACTIVITY

Study the table below.

Percentage of dependent children living in different family types
Great Britain

Great Britain	1972	1981	1991–92	Percentages 1998–99
Couple families				
1 child	16	18	17	15
2 children	35	41	37	36
3 or more children	41	29	27	26
Lone-mother families				
1 child	2	3	5	6
2 children	2	4	7	8
3 or more children	2	3	6	7
Lone-father families				
1 child	1	1	–	1
2 or more children	1	1	1	1
All dependent children	100	100	100	100

Source: *General Household Survey*, Office for National Statistics

1   What percentage of children lived in lone-parent families in 1998–99?

2   What is the percentage increase since 1972?

3   What is the percentage change in children living in couple families between 1972 and 1998–99?

4   Account for the changes you have identified.

5   What impact might these trends have on the services that need to be provided to support the family?

Further reading

Bell, J (1999) *Doing your research project*, Open University Press, Buckinghamshire
Denscombe, M (2001) *Sociology Update*, Olympus, Leicester
Green, S (2000) *Research methods*, Stanley Thornes, Cheltenham
Moore, S (1998) *Social welfare alive*, Stanley Thornes, Cheltenham
ONS (2000) *Social Trends*, The Stationery Office, London
ONS (1998) *Regional Trends*, The Stationery Office, London

Useful websites

www.updates.co.uk   *Sociology Update*
www.ons.gov.uk   Office for National Statistics

5 Media sources of information

In the last two chapters, we looked at different types of secondary information and how they can be used as part of the research process. Another very good source of information is the media: this includes newspapers, television and films. The advantage of media sources is that they are up to date as they are current information. Back copies of newspapers, magazines and journals will give you a flavour of the thoughts of that particular time.

This chapter covers how different media sources can be used in the research process. It also identifies some of the issues that you need to be aware of when using the media:

◆ Using the media for research

◆ What are the advantages of using the mass media?

◆ Classifying the newspapers

◆ How to use media sources effectively

◆ Other factors that affect the media viewpoint

◆ How to analyse material from media sources

◆ Scale and scope of media analysis

◆ Presenting and concluding results of research from media analysis

◆ Evaluating the effectiveness of research using media sources.

Using the media for research

Most research projects will allow you to use the media as a source of information at some point. The term 'media' is a very broad: it includes newspapers, magazines, television, radio and films. These are known as the 'mass media'. In addition, there are specialist publications, which are aimed at specific audiences. These are more difficult to get hold of but can be valuable in some research areas.

Fictional media such as plays, TV drama and film may also be used to gain data for research projects. The role of women at a particular point in history, for example, is often portrayed well in a fictional form, as are other health and social care related issues such as housing, health care and education. An example of this is the role of women as depicted in period dramas such as the movie *Far from the Madding Crowd*, based on the 19th-century novel by Thomas Hardy.

In a research project, media sources may be used in two ways:

1 **As an information source**. The media can provide useful background information on public debates through official and unofficial reports, e.g. statistics given on the television. They provide points of view on current issues. These views may differ from one media source to another, but that variation is valuable in itself as it helps researchers to weigh up the arguments. The media as an information source provides a useful foundation of fact and opinion.

2 **As a subject of research analysis**. A research project may require media analysis to investigate a topic area. For example, a research project looking at attitudes to private health care may decide to analyse how private health care is depicted in the media. In this case, the way the media work becomes an area of interest. Such an approach will focus more on how a topic is presented, and the issues of bias, as well as popular attitudes.

What are the advantages of using the mass media?

◆ Information is relatively easy to collect. There is an abundance of source material, depending on the area of research.

◆ Media sources are relatively cheap as a resource.

◆ Media material is widely available. Most towns have large newsagents which carry a wide range of different magazines and papers.

◆ They are a source of up-to-date information.

◆ They may be the only source of information available if you are investigating a very topical, current subject. It can take a long time before material becomes published in other sources, such as textbooks.

◆ The information is accessible to the audience. In general, media sources do not use the kind of technical language often found in specialist books. However, because different newspapers are aimed at different audiences, the nature of the language does vary in terms of complexity.

Classifying the newspapers

Newspapers are often categorised according to type, as indicated below. It is important to know what information you get from what type of newspaper and their treatment of it. The level of difficulty each paper presents can be identified through a language assessment test such as the one outlined in Chapter 9.

Types of paper	Readability level
Tabloid: *Sun, Mirror*	21
Middlebrow: Daily *Mail, Daily Express*	24
Broadsheet: *Guardian, Daily Telegraph, The Times*	38

ACTIVITY

Read the extracts from the three newspapers below:

'Emotionally exhausted' staff giving up on the NHS

One nurse in three 'is ready to resign'

By **Paul Kendall**
Technology Correspondent

MORE than a third of nurses in England are planning to leave the Health Service within a year because the workload has left them 'emotionally exhausted'.

The situation is even more serious among those under 30, with more than half saying they will resign within 12 months, according to an international study published today.

Researchers found that nurses in Germany obtain twice as much job satisfaction as their English counterparts, while three times as many Canadian nurses say they are happy with their pay.

Professor Linda Aiken of the University of Pennsylvania, which carried out the survey, said the findings exposed the shocking working conditions within the NHS.

'Nurses are simply overwhelmed,' she added.

'They are working extraordinarily hard to give everything they have to people who are sick. But the conditions in hospitals are undermining their best efforts.

'They are fighting against a system that desperately needs to be modernised.

'Nurses could be much more productive than they are at present and provide better care for patients if their working conditions were improved.'

Professor Aiken's findings – published in the journal Health Affairs – suggest the Government will find it very difficult to overcome the shortage of nurses in the NHS.

WHAT THEY THINK ABOUT THEIR JOB

	Per cent dissatisfied with present job	% with scores in high burnout range	% planning to leave present job in the next year
USA	41.0	43.2	22.7
Canada	32.9	36.0	16.6
England	36.1	36.2	38.9
Scotland	37.7	29.1	30.3
Germany	17.4	15.2	16.7

● Figures are per cent agreeing

	Are there enough nurses to provide quality care?	Are there enough staff to get the work done?	Are salaries adequate?
USA	34.4	33.4	57.0
Canada	35.2	37.4	69.0
England	29.0	28.4	19.9
Scotland	38.1	30.3	25.9
Germany	36.5	37.7	40.5

Vacancies have risen from 7,300 in 1999 to 22,000 this year.

Research published by the Royal College of Nursing (RCN) last year suggested 110,000 nurses will leave the NHS by 2004.

Nurses surveyed in the international study – 5,000 in England and 4,700 in Scotland – said the staff shortage was affecting patient care.

More than two thirds of nurses in England said there were not enough staff 'to get the work done' while fewer than one in three felt the quality of care on their unit was excellent.

The large number of vacancies is stopping qualified nurses from seeking extra training and learning the latest techniques and treatments.

Professor Aiken also high-

lighted the large number of young nurses planning to leave the profession as a cause for concern – especially with so many nurses in the NHS nearing retirement age.

The number aged over 50 has risen by 35 per cent in the last decade, with almost a quarter

'Unique insight'

of all nurses now over 50. 'This points to a worsening nursing shortage in the future,' said the professor.

An RCN spokesman described the study's findings as 'worrying'. She added: 'The UK is currently experiencing its worst nursing shortage with 22,000 current vacancies. This

research supports the RCN's own evidence on the concerns of nurses about the impact of nurse shortages on the quality of patient care.'

Professor Aiken surveyed more than 43,000 registered nurses in 711 hospitals in England, Scotland, Canada, Germany and the U.S.

Fewer than one in five nurses in Germany said they were dissatisfied with their job.

More than half of those in the U.S. and more than two-thirds in Canada said their salaries were 'adequate'.

A spokesman for the Department of Health said 7,500 nurses had returned to the NHS since 1999, when the survey was carried out.

Comment – Page TEN
p.kendall@dailymail.co.uk

Byers to promise leave for adoptive parents

By Nigel Morris
Political Correspondent

PARENTS WHO adopt are to be promised new rights that the Government says will leave them up to £2,600 better off. The pledge will come this week as Stephen Byers, the Secretary of State for Trade and Industry, fleshes out plans to extend paternity leave.

Under the scheme, working parents who adopt will be brought into line with birth parents by gaining the entitlement to six months of paid leave and six of unpaid leave. If both parents are in jobs, one will be able to claim the statutory time off work, while the other will be able to take two weeks of paid leave.

A DTI source said adoptive parents, who currently have no right to any paid leave, will gain up to £2,600 as a result of the move starting in 2003. "Mr Byers believes that in the past there has been a failure to recognise and support the vital role that adoptive parents play. That is why the Government is proposing a new deal," the source said. The source added that childcare experts recommend one parent stay at home for the first few months of the placement to make it a success.

Mr Byers will also confirm moves to entitle about 450,000 new fathers a year to two weeks' paid leave. They will have to have been with their employer for six months and take the fortnight in a single block within two months of their child's birth.

Small businesses will be able to reclaim the amount they pay and will receive extra compensation.

The DTI source said: "Women are more likely to return to work if their partner has taken paternity leave. This new right will give fathers the opportunity to support their partner when they most need it but with minimum disruption to their employer's business."

The moves were announced in the Budget by Gordon Brown, the Chancellor, in March. Mr Byers will publish two documents that explain how the plan will work in practice.

SHOPPING MAUL

Stores losing out as we find new ways to spend our cash

EXCLUSIVE by CLINTON MANNING, Business Editor

STORES are suffering a slump as customers lose the urge to shop till they drop, a survey yesterday revealed.

Although we have much more spare cash than 20 years ago, far less of it is going into high street tills. In 1980, we blew 47 per cent of our disposable income in the shops. That figure has now dropped to just below 33 per cent.

And the survey into shopping habits predicts the figure will fall to under 30 per cent by 2005.

Richard Hyman, chairman of Verdict Research which carried out the survey, said there was a seismic change going on in the high street.

People were shopping less often, visiting fewer stores on each trip and demanding more for their money.

Mr Hyman said: "It is too strong to say shopping is out of fashion, but we don't have the same urge to shop till we drop.

"Consumers have got a whole host of other things to spend their money on.

"They are eating out more, taking more holidays and going to the movies more often.

"Mobile phones, computer games, even pensions and private health care are eating up more of our time and money."

He added: "The current retail climate is the toughest we have ever seen outside a recession."

Mr Hyman said: "It's up to the stores to convince us we want the things they stock."

Mark Bradshaw, deputy director general of the British Retail Consortium, agreed these were challenging times.

He said: "But retailers remain dynamic and will stay ahead of the pack by sticking to the golden rule – the customer is king."

WHAT WE SPEND OUR MONEY ON

Eating out · Holidays · Movies · Mobile phones · Computer games · Pensions

1   Carry out a readability test on each extract, as explained Chapter 9 (page 152). Which type of newspaper do you think each extract comes from?

2   What other factors in the articles indicate their source?

3   Do the articles have a particular emphasis in the way they present the information?

4   Which do you feel most comfortable with and why?

5   What factors do you need to be aware of when using this type of material?

Costs

Individually, media sources are relatively cheap – newspapers cost less than a pound to just over a pound, television programmes are freely available, apart for the cost of a licence fee, TV programmes can be videoed, and videos of film can be rented. However, in large-scale research, the costs can mount up if it involves access to a large number of media sources over a period of time.

A useful source of information is the local library, where a number of different newspapers and magazines are available each day. These are then archived for a certain period of time – generally depending on the size of the library. This will allow you to research articles from both present and past publications. If required, key articles can be photocopied to put in the appendices of the research to support the findings.

Older material is also available on CD-ROM, which libraries usually stock. The advantage of CD-ROMs is that you can use the computer to search for specific information, saving you from having to read or scan all the material to find what you want.

Old films and television programmes may also be accessed from film archives, such as the British Film Institute.

ACTIVITY

Visit your local library. Choose a CD-ROM for a newspaper and do a search on the following topics:

- Smoking and adolescents
- Coronary heart disease
- Prescription costs.

What sort of information did you find?

How to use media sources effectively

Although it is relatively easy to collect material from media sources, it is more difficult to make it into meaningful information.

To make good use of such material, you must plan well and give considerable thought to the approach you will take for analysis. Generally, media analysis takes a lot of time. It is important that you check the material for the bias or personal viewpoint of the writer. Bias can be identified in a number of ways; for example, when a balanced view of an argument is not given.

Political bias

It is well known that many newspapers have a particular political preference and that this is reflected in the way they report and comment on issues and stories. This is generally most obvious in the editor's column. It is important that this is recognised in any analysis that is done. However, newspapers do publish articles by renowned journalists which may reflect a view different from that of the editor, so look out for these.

Choice of language

You can also draw conclusions about the way an author or reporter views issues from the language they choose to describe or explain an issue. The choice of language can change the tone and strength of meaning in an article; and this choice is entirely that of the author/reporter.

Below are some examples of the way the media uses language to highlight issues:

24-hour drinking 'will lead to huge rise in violence'

Regular breast screening cuts risk by 60%

Ecstasy super pill kills girl

Choose two newspapers published today from the different 'types' of newspapers.

◆ *Using a story which is reported in both papers, make a list of words which give an indication of how the reporters feel about the issue. These may be words used to provoke a reaction or dramatise the issue.*

◆ *Are the stories reported in the same way in both papers?*

◆ *How far does the language suggest a particular opinion in both cases?*

Other factors that influence the media viewpoint

Other factors that affect what a paper publishes include:

◆ the owner's interests

◆ legal issues which can prevent information being published

◆ national security issues which prevent publication of certain information

◆ the public mood – newspapers are sensitive to the public mood and this may influence the way they present information, or if they print it at all.

Whatever media source you use, it is important that you support the information in the media with statistics where possible. This helps strengthen the work. Sources such as *Social Trends* will allow you to check statistics quoted in the media.

It is important to recognise that often newspapers conduct 'surveys' of their own and present the information as valid data. This data is likely to contain bias. It is not always clear how the data has been collected or the sample chosen. It is essential that this 'data' is treated with care.

When using data, it is important that you quote the source and date of publication as well as any concerns you may have about the information in terms of representativeness, validity and reliability. It is not uncommon for media sources to be one-sided, but this is not generally a problem as long as it is recognised in the use of the material.

Always be clear about who is writing and the audience they are aiming it at. Highlight any bias, issues or points that have been left out.

How to analyse material from media sources

Analysing content is an organised way of identifying specific issues or activities that appear in the media. It is a quantitative research method and essentially records how often, how many and how much. You may also look at where an issue is reported – whether on the front page or in the middle – as well as looking at how much space is devoted to it. These can be a measure of the importance of a story. How to analyse is a careful decision which needs to be made.

It is important that your approach is well thought through and carried out carefully in an ordered manner. What you choose to analyse will depend on the issue you are researching. Once decided, it is essential that you apply the same criteria throughout the analysis. Any change midway through will make your results unreliable and have less meaning.

Therefore, it is essential that you decide at the start of the exercise on the categories you will use for the media analysis, and that you will not change these. To do this effectively you will need to spend time deciding on the categories. Then it is essential you trial these on at least one source being analysed. This will:

◆ ensure all the appropriate criteria have been covered

◆ ensure you are clear about what your criteria actually cover – detailed written explanations should be kept

◆ allow expansion of the criteria or the discarding of inappropriate categories before carrying out the major exercise.

An example of a media analysis sheet is given below.

Media analysis sheet				
Portrayal of caring roles in the media				
The gender for which the role applies	**The activities being undertaken**	**Main tasks**	**Skills being demonstrated**	**Adult or child demonstrating the role**
Females only	Cleaning Nursing	Vacuuming Looking after sick child	Domestic Caring	Adult Adult
Males only				
Both sexes				

ACTIVITY

Choose a popular soap opera on television and try out the analysis, using the chart above.

◆   How well does it work?

◆   What conclusions could you draw from this exercise?

◆   What changes would you like to see in the categories?

◆   How could you adapt this to use with newspapers?

The complexity of the sheet will depend on the issue being analysed. Newspapers and magazines can be analysed in a similar way. An example of a magazine analysis is given below.

An analysis of the images of women in adverts in women's magazines

Catagory of analysis	Magazine 1	Magazine 2
Date of edition analysed	July 2001	July 3rd 2001
Frequency of magazine	Monthly	Weekly
Market segment	Mature women	Younger women
Type of magazine	General lifestyle	Health
Price	£2.70	£1.90
Number of pages	216	135
Number of pages of adverts	75	44
Numbers depicting women	23	30
Analysis of images by age		
< 35 years	20	30
35–65 years	3	
> 65 years		
Analysis by body mass		
Slim	23	30
Overweight	0	0
Product being advertised		
Beauty	15	25
Household	4	1

Using this style of analysis, you can identify and analyse whatever categories you wish. You can also analyse as many different types of magazines as you feel necessary. It is often useful to analyse them on the same chart as this allows you to carry out an easy comparison and will help you to draw out conclusions.

Scale and scope of media analysis

There is so much media material that any analysis has the potential to be very large. You may find that you have far too much material to deal with, making the task too large and cumbersome to be able to complete.

It is important to remember how much time you have available. You will probably also have to limit the scope of the work to reduce the amount of material being examined. This can be done in several ways, while retaining the required focus.

1 Limit the number of sources, by taking representative samples. For example, as previously stated, newspapers are categorised into three groups: tabloid or popular, middlebrow, and broadsheet or quality. To limit sources, you could decide to analyse one paper from each category, assuming it gives representation of others in that group.

2 Limit the time span of the research. Decide to look at media sources over a specific time span – obviously the smaller the time frame, the less material you will need to analyse. Examples may include:

   ◆ women's magazines over one week

   ◆ newspapers on one day

   ◆ advertisements between TV programmes over a given time.

Any of these will still give plenty of material, which you may wish to narrow down even further. This could be achieved by surveying the most 'popular' reading materials and narrowing your focus that way.

3 Have a specific focus, such as looking at an issue in a particular type of media, e.g. the popular press only.

It is important to justify how you chose to limit your scope for analysis in terms of the research being carried out. An arbitrary decision about choice of material without justification has the potential to make the research invalid.

When limiting the range of sources, you need to ensure that you do not make sweeping statements in your conclusions. You cannot claim that all popular papers are against private health care for example, if you have analysed only one paper on one day. Your choice of language will be important. You can state, 'From my research, it appears that the popular press does not support private health care', but you must recognise the limitations of your work and how this may distort your conclusions.

Presenting and concluding results of research from media analysis

Media analysis takes specific aspects and looks at them out of the context in which they have been written. In doing this, some of the detail and meaning will be lost as this is a broad analysis rather than a specific one. You will need to comment on this when you conclude your results and make sure you highlight how this could affect those results. It will also be useful to comment on it when you evaluate the work.

Presenting results

Results may be most effectively presented as tables, which are a clear way of presenting a lot of information. A table allows the reader to see clearly the full results of the analysis that has been carried out.

It will also be necessary to draw conclusions from your results, to make sense of what you have discovered through the analysis. If possible, you should then compare your results with other research of a similar nature, or to theories that you have found in texts during your research. This will allow you to conclude whether your findings are similar to or very different from any work that has gone before.

It is important to remember that your research is likely to be on a smaller scale than other published material, and this should be reflected in any comments.

Evaluating the effectiveness of research using media sources

The evaluation should show that you recognise the strengths and weaknesses of your work and that you appreciate the effect they may have had on your findings.

In the evaluation, you should critically evaluate your choices of media material, assessing the extent to which it is representative of the range available. You should also evaluate the choice of categories you have chosen to analyse the material and the extent to which they enabled you to analyse what you set out to do. Identify any difficulties that arose during the categorisation exercise and state how these may have affected the results, or explain how you dealt with the issue to ensure reliability was maintained.

It is important to recognise any changes you would make to the approach used and discuss the potential value these would have had on the finished work.

Most evaluations identify how the piece of work could be continued if the work is to be extended further.

Read the article from the *Daily Telegraph* below called 'Middle-class children more prone to allergies'.

Middle-class children more prone to allergies

By David Derbyshire, Medical Correspondent

CHILDREN from middle class families are more likely to develop asthma and eczema than those from less affluent backgrounds, research has shown.

Campaigners said the clean and cossetted indoor way of life of more affluent children — which shields them from bacteria needed to prime their immune systems — could be to blame.

A study of 1,300 children found that it was those with the wealthiest parents who were significantly more likely to suffer from allergic conditions.

This finding backs up previous studies, and international health statistics, which suggest that allergies are a disease of wealthy Western lifestyles.

Scientists who presented the latest findings yesterday said they were puzzled why youngsters were more likely to fall victim to allergies if their parents were wealthier.

The study, presented at the Congress of the European Academy of Allergology and Clinical Immunology in Lisbon, compared the socio-economic status and medical history of 1,314 German children.

Prof Ulrich Wahn, specialist in paediatric medicine at Humboldt University, in Berlin, said: "It is very confusing.

"These are middle class parents, who have taken on board the need for a healthy lifestyle; low rates of smoking in pregnancy, low rates of smoking in the home and low levels of pet ownership, together with high rates of breastfeeding, which are five times that of mothers with a low socio-economic status.

"We cannot work out what they are doing wrong. There is clearly an unidentified factor that is so strong it can overcome all the lifestyle changes we encourage parents to adopt."

The multi-allergy study is now following the children, who were born in 1990, into their teens to try to identify the mystery factor.

Muriel Simmons, chief executive of the British Allergy Foundation, said: "What seems to be emerging is that children who are not exposed to bacteria are more at risk of developing allergies.

"We have developed lifestyles where our homes are ultra-clean, where children who are well off play on computers rather than getting into rough and tumble in the mud outdoors, where they get cuts and bruises and get used to fighting off infection.

"The children of farmers and those on lower incomes are more likely to have to think up their own fun and play outdoors than the children whose parents can afford computers and are afraid to let them outdoors."

British scientists are looking at a technique which could see children injected with bacteria in an attempt to prime their immune systems.

The number of children under five who suffer from asthma in Britain has almost doubled in the past decade, from 11·3 per cent in 1990 to 21·3 per cent in 1998. Food allergies are also on the increase.

1   Summarise the main points of the article.

2   Why might it be a useful piece of research for an investigation on allergies in children?

3   How could you use the information in a research context?

Summary

Media sources provide a wealth of information about a wide range of topics. They often provide the most up-to-date thinking on an issue and are therefore a valuable source for research.

When selecting media sources, the huge extent of the material available means that most researchers will need to be selective in what they use. This means they will need to identify a sample of sources and be able to justify their choice in terms of the focus of the work.

Analysis of media material takes time and planning is essential in order to ensure reliability and validity.

3

Primary research methods

6 Questionnaires

A questionnaire is one of the most popular research methods. It is a key way of finding answers to questions for a research project. Many people believe it is easy to design and carry out a questionnaire, but this is not the case. Designing an effective questionnaire is difficult. A lot of effort and time may be needed to ensure you are asking the right questions, in the right way, in order to get the information needed. It takes considerable skill.

This chapter aims to explain how to design an effective questionnaire, highlighting the common pitfalls that need to be avoided. The chapter includes:

◆ What is a questionnaire?

◆ Types of questionnaire

◆ Devising a good questionnaire

◆ Designing the questionnaire

◆ Deciding on your sample

◆ Devising questions for a questionnaire

◆ Organising a questionnaire

◆ Piloting the questionnaire

◆ Collating and analysing the results

◆ Evaluating a questionnaire.

What is a questionnaire?

Essentially, a questionnaire is a printed form of questions designed by a researcher, which is given to potential respondents to answer. In general, a questionnaire is not completed with a researcher present.

Questionnaires are often used because they give a broad response to a subject. However, they do not provide much depth to the subject; this is best gained through interviews. Interview techniques are explained in Chapter 7.

A questionnaire is quantitative research, in that it can provide lots of responses relatively easily. It is a good way of asking a large number of people straightforward questions.

It is not as expensive to carry out as interviews, since the researcher does not need to be present when the questionnaire is completed. Therefore, the man-hours are fewer. However, it does take time to collate and analyse the large number of responses that are gained.

Types of questionnaire

There are several different types of questionnaire. The most common ones are:

◆ **Postal questionnaires.** These are questionnaires sent out and returned by post. This is the cheapest form of research. However, it can produce errors in the results as you have no way of knowing who has returned the questionnaire.

◆ **Telephone questionnaires.** This is doing research over the telephone by asking people certain questions. You read out the questions and list possible responses if there is a choice to be made. You record the responses given. The advantage of this method is the immediate response you get.

◆ **Self-completion questionnaires.** The questionnaire is given to the respondent, who completes it and returns it as required. This gives you less control over the response rate, but gives the respondents the opportunity to complete it in their own time, so responses may be more considered.

Devising a good questionnaire

Designing a good questionnaire involves going through a number of stages. You need to go through each stage to ensure you design a questionnaire that draws out the information you need.

Pre-construction issues

There are a few points to consider before you design the questionnaire.

◆ Keep the questionnaire brief. It is important that you bear in mind the length of the questionnaire from the outset. Long questionnaires tend to discourage potential respondents from filling them in. Keep it brief, and ask only what you need to ask. For example, if you don't need to know the age and gender of respondents, then don't ask these questions.

◆ Think about the presentation. A complicated and wordy questionnaire is more likely to be discarded by the respondent. People will be put off by having to read what appears to be a lot of text, and on things they see as 'non-essential'. Therefore, when designing the questionnaire, it is important to:
  – make the layout attractive
  – leave plenty of space around each question as this gives the appearance of fewer words.

◆ Position the boxes for responses on the right-hand side of the page, given that we read from left to right. For example:

How many pieces of fruit do you eat in a day? [   ]

[   ] How many pieces of fruit do you eat in a day?

You can see how having the boxes on the right-hand side makes it far easier for the respondent to complete.

Designing the questionnaire
Planning

From the very start you need to be clear about what you want the questionnaire to find out. This will ensure that you get the information that you need for your research.

To do this, you need to research your topic thoroughly before you start. You do this by researching secondary source material such as textbooks and media articles. This will give you a good foundation on which to build your questionnaire. The research should help direct you towards what you hope to find out and will also give you something to compare your results with when you analyse them.

Sometimes there is no previously published material available on the area to be investigated. For example, if you want to investigate consumer attitudes towards beef during the initial stages of the BSE scare. In such cases, you need to consider your line of enquiry even more carefully to ensure you are clear about the purpose of your questionnaire.

Deciding on your sample

Who are you going to ask? Questionnaires need to be valid and reliable. To be valid means that the questionnaire has to be accurately focused, and that it asks questions which find out what it sets out to find out. Reliable means that the research method used is appropriate for the information it intends to find out.

To ensure your questionnaire is valid and reliable, you will need to decide on a sample frame. A sample frame is the people you will target the questionnaire to and how many you will ask. There are many different types of sample, and the choice you make will vary according to the aim of the questionnaire within the scope of the overall research.

Different types of sampling methods

There are various sampling methods that can be used in research.

Random sample

In this sample, respondents are chosen at random – almost as a lottery, or out of a hat. Everyone on the list has an equal chance of being chosen. For example, if you wanted to ask a sample of ten students from an early years class about their experiences on work placement, you could put all their names into a box and pick out a sample of ten. In this way everyone has an equal chance of being chosen.

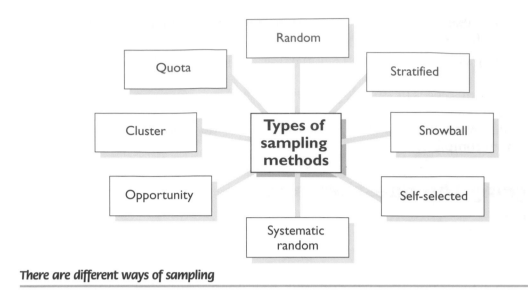

There are different ways of sampling

Stratified sample

This is a sample which reflects a particular age and/or culture of the cohort. A cohort is the total group of people you could ask. For example, the sixth-form class given in the example below would be a cohort.

Therefore, you need to analyse the age and cultural groups of the potential respondents and then ensure your sample reflects this.

Look at this example from a survey on researching the views of sixth-formers in a school or college on smoking. The cohort is all the students. There are 360 in the sixth form, all from the same cultural group. Their gender and year groups were divided up as follows:

Year	Numbers	Number of males (%)	Number of females (%)	% of total number in cohort
Year 12	180	100 (56)	80 (44)	50
Year 13	140	70 (50)	70 (50)	39
Year 14	40	30 (75)	10 (25)	11

If you were going to take a 33% sample (120 students), you would divide the allocation of the questionnaires as follows.

Year	% of sample	Number of questionnaire	Number of males	Number of females
Year 12	50	60	34	26
Year 13	39	46	23	23
Year 14	11	14	10	4

This is the sample frame. By doing this, the researcher can ensure that every group is represented in the appropriate proportions. This sample reflects the structure of the full body of students in the sixth form. It can then be assumed that any findings could be reflective of all students.

This careful calculation takes time but it is useful in that any results can be seen as representative of the group being investigated.

It becomes even more complicated if you include consideration of ethnic origin or culture as categories across the age group.

ACTIVITY

Using the cohort of sixth-formers given above, devise a sample frame where there are cultural differences in the year groups as follows.

Year	Total number of students from ethnic cultures	Number of males	Number of females
Year 12	90	50	40
Year 13	30	10	20
Year 13	6	4	2

1   What will the sample frame look like now?

2   Do you think that making this distinction may affect the results?

3   Do you think such an exercise is necessary with all questionnaires?

If you want to be able to compare the results across the males and females or the cultures, you will need to be able to distinguish who completed which questionnaire. This will need to be done in a way so that full anonymity is not lost. If the respondents feel they can be identified as 'individuals', they may be more reluctant to be fully honest in their answers. This is particularly important when a sample is small, as they are more easily identifiable.

You can identify groups by:

◆ distributing questionnaires photocopied on different coloured paper. This works well if the samples in each subsection of the sample frame are large.

◆ coding each questionnaire with a code to reflect the subsection of the cohort they are questioning. Year 12 female may be coded Y12F; Year 13 male for an ethnic group may be coded Y13ME. This allows all the questionnaires to be copied on the same colour paper, and respondents are less likely to be concerned about being identified.

Quota sample

This type of sampling is where you choose the number of respondents you want from each category before the start. You then give out questionnaires at random until you have covered the stated number.

Cluster sample

This is a type of sampling where the researcher chooses a particular group of people who are located in a particular area for a specific reason. An example may be people who live in a specific street or all students in a particular group.

Such a sample is generally chosen because there is a specific reason for doing so, such as work specifically focusing on that area.

In this type of sampling frame, you are likely to question all of the target group.

Opportunity sample

This sample consists of anyone who passes by a particular point when the research is being carried out. There is no selecting done by the researcher, as all who happen to pass by are given a questionnaire and included in the sample.

Systematic random sample

This is a structured sample where the researcher chooses respondents in an organised manner. They generally have a list of people, such as an electoral role or a register. They then choose every so many people on the list, e.g. every sixth person.

Self-selected sample

This method is where people volunteer to take part. Sometimes, incentives, such as prizes, are offered to encourage people to do this.

This does mean, however, that you will attract a particular type of person, so your results may be affected.

Snowball sample

This is another form of selection whereby the sample selects itself through word of mouth. Respondents put themselves forward to take part in the questionnaire.

Whichever method you choose to select your sample, it is important you identify your reason for choosing the method in your writing up of the research. Most samples will be a balance between the ideal sample and what is practical and available. The choice is likely to be affected by cost, time and resource limitations, but as long as this is recognised in the analysis of the results and the evaluation, then it is reasonable.

Preamble

It is important that you explain the purpose of any questionnaire at the start. This ensures that the respondent is aware of what you are trying to do and why. This can also encourage the potential respondent to participate, as they can see there is a use or value in doing it. Also you must ensure complete confidentiality, and this will encourage more people to complete it.

Explaining how long it will take to complete the questionnaire will also encourage more people to complete it.

It is common to explain how the results of the research will be used. Look at this example.

Please would you complete this questionnaire on your diet in pregnancy. Your responses will help in research I am carrying out for my BTEC National Diploma in Childhood Studies. All responses are treated in confidence and your name is not necessary. The questions should take about five minutes to complete. This information that I gather will be written up in my research project.

Other information that must be given at the start of the questionnaire includes:

◆ Instructions on how to fill out the questionnaire. It is important to tell the respondents that they must use pen or pencil if the questionnaire is to be read by an optical mark reader. An optical mark reader is a machine which reads questionnaires and collates the results.

◆ Details of the deadline, if applicable, so the respondents know when they need to send it back by.

◆ How to return the questionnaire. If it is to be returned by post, include a stamped-addressed envelope to ensure a good response rate, especially if the questionnaire has a tight deadline. People are reluctant to spend money on an envelope and a stamp for the sake of someone else.

It is important that return details are clear and relatively straightforward, as anything which requires respondents to go out of their way is likely to reduce the return rate. A response rate to a questionnaire is usually below 24%, so clarity is almost as important a requirement as the design of the questionnaire itself.

One way to improve the response rate is to wait whilst the respondents complete the questionnaires there and then. However, this may not always be practical, and can influence the response received.

Devising questions for a questionnaire

Writing good questions for questionnaires requires skill. The questions need to be clear to ensure that the respondents understand what is being asked, and phrased in such a way as to ensure you get them to focus on the area of interest. It is easy to compose a question you think will cover the area you want it to, but those completing the questionnaire may read it in a completely different way. Therefore, it is worth spending some time thinking about your questions to ensure they are right before going to print. Test them on other people to see if they understand the questions and can answer them.

There are several points to bear in mind when designing a questionnaire. These will help you avoid the potential pitfalls.

I Relevance

Make sure that the questions are relevant to what you want to find out. Questions on age, gender and occupation are common on questionnaires, but you need to consider whether this information is relevant to your study. The rule is, if the question is not relevant to the study, then leave it out.

Respondents give up their time to answer questionnaires, and irrelevant questions are likely to discourage them.

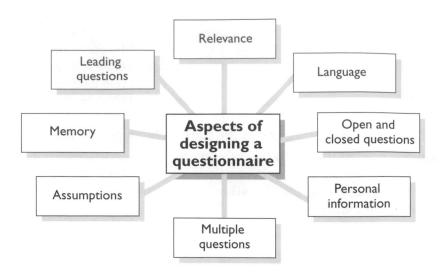

What to keep in mind when designing a questionnaire

2 Language

Think carefully about the language you use and the people you are targeting the questionnaire at. Choose straightforward words that people will understand. Respondents do not want to have to use a dictionary to decipher the meaning of a question before they can answer it.

For example:

'What is the incidence of fried potato snack consumption in your establishment in one day?'

Can also be written as:

'How many packets of crisps are eaten in your house in one day?'

People are also not likely to answer a question if it looks complicated.

3 Open questions vs closed questions

Open questions

Open questions are those which allow free response by the respondent. They usually start with a 'wh' word, such as who, what, when, or why. An example of an open question is:

'What do you feel is the most effective way of improving the nation's health?'

Such questions will elicit a wide range of responses and can make analysis more difficult. However, they do give a more personal insight into the respondents' thoughts. This type of question is useful if you are unsure about the range of possible responses you may get.

Closed questions

Closed questions elicit more limited responses. They generally require a Yes or No answer, or there are a number of predetermined responses for the respondent to choose from.

For example:

Do you recycle your rubbish?   Yes / No

Such questions are useful if you are covering facts or where it is reasonable to guess the range of possible responses.

They are also easier for the respondent to complete as they often involve only ticking a box rather than writing an answer.

Tick the response which you think gives the correct answer.
Is fish a good source of:
a protein   [ ]
b fibre   [ ]
c vitamin C   [ ]
d fat   [ ]

They are also useful for questions where you need to categorise age or time into sections which are easy to analyse.

How often do you attend this gym?
a every day   [ ]
b twice a week   [ ]
c once per week   [ ]
d once a fortnight [ ]
e once a month   [ ]
or
Please state which age group you fall into
<19 [ ]   19–35 [ ]   36–50 [ ]   51–65 [ ]   >65 [ ]

Remember, when classifying age groups there shouldn't be any cross-over in the age spans. The groups should be as the example above and not 18, 18–35, 35–50, 50–65, and so on, as those who are 18, 35 or 50 will not know which category to tick.

Closed questions are far easier to analyse and results can be more effectively presented as graphs and charts. Such presentation can enhance the work and clarify the findings for the reader.

If you are going to use pre-selected responses, it is important that you think about these to ensure that they have clear meaning and that they are sufficiently different for the respondent to be able to make a definite choice.

How do you rate your doctor's performance?
Poor   [ ]
Average   [ ]
Good   [ ]

Each respondent will have a different measurement of poor, average and good. It is difficult to make comparisons as one person's 'good' will be another person's 'average'. The statements are not quantifiable enough. Other words which lack clear meaning include reasonable and adequate.

EXAMPLE

How do you rate the service provided by the surgery?

Adequate   [   ]

Reasonable   [   ]

Good   [   ]

Poor   [   ]

Again, each individual will have a different interpretation of these terms. There may also be confusion over adequate and reasonable, as both tend to say the same thing.

You should also consider the order the responses are given in so that they are logical. It could be suggested that the order should be good, then adequate and finally poor.

It may be better to quantify opinions on the quality of the service in a different way.

EXAMPLE

Are the surgery opening hours:

Too long   [   ]

Too short   [   ]

Suitable   [   ]

How do you find the arrangements for making an appointment?

Well organised, efficient, no delays   [   ]

Good organisation but some delay   [   ]

Poor, frequent delays   [   ]

Coding closed questions

Closed questions are often pre-coded to make analysis easier and quicker. Each potential response is given a code so that it is not necessary to record the answers in full every time an individual responds.

EXAMPLE

Using the start of a questionnaire to college students

1 Gender

Male [   ] **A**   Female [   ] **B**

2 Years at the college

1st year [ ] **A** 2nd year [ ] **B** 3rd year [ ] **C**

3 Course of study

AVCE [ ] **A**

A levels [ ] **B**

GCSE resits [ ] **C**

GNVQ Intermediate [ ] **D**

4 How far has the course met your expectations?

Fully [ ]

Partly [ ]

Not at all [ ]

The codes are then transferred to a summary sheet or table where columns can easily be totalled for analysis.

Respondent	1 Gender		2 Years			3 Course				4 Expectations		
	A	**B**	**A**	**B**	**C**	**A**	**B**	**C**	**D**	**A**	**B**	**C**
1												
2												
3												
4												

It would be beneficial to do this as a database as this would enable you to manipulate the data during the analysis stage. It would also allow the data to be sorted so you could compare male and female responses, or how many in the 3rd year were fully satisfied with their courses compared with those in 1st year.

4 Personal information

Respondents are more likely to complete personal information, such as age or income, if placed in a range rather than having to give exact information. Therefore, closed questions are best for this type of question.

EXAMPLE

Is your gross income bracket, per annum:

≤£10,000 [ ] £10,001–£20,000 [ ] £20,001–£30,000 [ ] £30,001 + [ ] ?

Remember, people do not like giving out personal information, so ask only if it is absolutely relevant and necessary for the research. This should also be obvious to the respondents.

If you do need to ask personal information, it is often suggested that such questions should be put at the end of the questionnaire. Putting them at the beginning risks offending the respondent who may not then complete the questionnaire. If they are at the end, the respondent will by then have completed most of the questionnaire, and may think, 'Why not?', and complete it. If the respondent chooses not to complete it, you at least have the information from the rest of the completed questionnaire.

5 Multiple questions

Make sure the questions ask respondents for only one answer. Avoid asking a question that is really more than one question. An example is:

'Did you breast or bottle feed and why did you choose this method of infant feeding?'

With such cases, respondents may answer only the second part of the question, and this will reduce the reliability of your results.

If both parts of the question are important, it is better to break the question into parts (a) and (b) or make them two very separate questions.

EXAMPLE

1a Did you breast or bottle feed?

Breast   [ ]

Bottle   [ ]

b Why did you choose this method of infant feeding?...

....

....

Breaking up a question into separate parts will ensure that all respondents are clearly directed into answering all questions.

6 Assumptions

Try to avoid questions that make presumptions about the opinions or actions of the respondent. This also applies to knowledge and experiences. A question such as 'How long did you smoke?' assumes all respondents have smoked. Likewise, 'Which foreign countries did you visit on your holiday this year?' assumes all respondents have holidays abroad.

You need to be sure that every question asks something that the respondent can reasonably answer.

7 Memory

Most people have short memories for detail. Therefore, do not ask people for information about something which happened five or ten years before. Most people may be reasonably expected to remember up to one year before with relative accuracy.

For example, it would be impossible for most people to answer the question 'When did you read your first book without adult help?'

If you need to try to find out information from the past, you are likely to need memory joggers such as special events about the time. In this case, interviews are probably a better research method than a questionnaire.

ACTIVITY

Ask people to recall their diet over the last week. Ask them to note down everything they ate and drank.

1   How accurately do they remember?

2   When does their memory get hazy?

3   How would they manage if you asked them to note down everything eaten over the last month?

Unless you are asking about significant events which people will remember easily, use memory joggers to help people think about where they were and what they were doing. Remember that memory is poor.

8 Leading questions

It is easy to devise questions which suggest a preferred response, particularly if the questionnaire designer feels a particular way.

EXAMPLE

Should the cruel and heartless sport of fox hunting be banned?	
Yes	[ ]
No	[ ]

This can lead to bias in the answers you receive. Therefore, it is important that you check your questions rigorously for this before you send out your questionnaire.

Routing questions

Sometimes you want to ask a question where the response given will affect the next question you want the person to answer. For example, if you asked the question,

---

1 Do you recycle your rubbish?

Yes   [ ]

No   [ ]

You would want to follow up with different questions depending on the answer. A 'Yes' could be followed up with:

2 What do you recycle?

Glass	[ ]
Plastic	[ ]
Paper	[ ]

Other, please state ....

Whereas a 'No' response might be followed up with:

3 Why don't you recycle?

Too much trouble	[ ]
No local recycling centre	[ ]
No car to take it to the recycling centre	[ ]
Too time consuming	[ ]

Other, please state ....

The easiest way to direct the respondent to the appropriate question is to 'route' them. Routing is where you direct the respondent to the next question by the choice of answer given in the previous one.

For example:

Do you recycle rubbish?

Yes	[ ] Go to question 2
No	[ ] Go to question 3

This ensures that respondents answer only questions which are relevant to them.

As you can see, designing a questionnaire is not a simple process. It takes a lot of skill and thought to get it right. It is very easy to make mistakes.

ACTIVITY

Study the questionnaire below.

Try to identify the faults in it. Some of the questions contain more than one question. There are at least 17 faults.

Questionnaire

Thank you for completing this short questionnaire on children's reading habits. For yor convenience, please leave the completed questionnaires in the staf room and I will collect them on my next placement day.

Part A : Personnel

1.   Name
2. Age
3. Quallifications
4. Nursery
5. Current position

[   ]

Part B : Your children

6. How many of the children in your nursery maintain concentration for the afternoon story and how many choose books as part of free play activity?

7. How supportive are parents in terms of encouraging their children to look at books at home?
   Very supportive
   Not very supportive
   Reasonable supportive
   Unhelpful
   Very unhelpful

8. How many parents normally attend parents' evening?

9. What use do you make of parents in the nursery?

10. How would you evaluate the book stock and arrangements in the nursery for book use?
    Poor
    Average
    Good

11. If you worked in London, how do you think things might be different?

12. Please tick the type of book most children prefer (tick only one) :
    a. a book with pictures   [   ]
    b. a story book   [   ]
    c. a factual book   [   ]
    d. a familiar story e.g. the three bears   [   ]
    e. Other; please state ....

Thank you for your co-operation. The next phase of this research involves the interviewing of a sample of respondents. If you do not wish to be further involved, please put a cross in the box above.

Comments on Questionnaire

Questionnaire

Assumes people will take part

Spelling

Thank you for completing this short questionnaire on children's reading habits. For yor convenience, please leave the completed questionnaires in the staf room and I will collect them on my next placement day.

• Spelling
• Not confidential

Part A : Personnel

1.   Name   *Not in line*

2. Age ← *Personal – is this necessary?*

3. Quallifications ← *Spelling*

4. Nursery

5. Current position

[   ] ← *Box is not near instruction linked to it*

Part B : Your children

6. How many of the children in your nursery maintain concentration for the afternoon story and how many choose books as part of free play activity?

Multiple question – better as two separate questions

7. How supportive are parents in terms of encouraging their children to look at books at home?

How would respondents know this?

Very poor order

Very supportive
Not very supportive
Reasonable supportive ← *Vague definitions*
Unhelpful
Very unhelpful

Memory – can people really remember this

8. How many parents normally attend parents' evening?

9. What use do you make of parents in the nursery? ← *Assumes parents are used*

10. How would you evaluate the book stock and arrangements in the nursery for book use?

Multiple question

Poor
Average ← *Definition will vary with each respondent*
Good

11. If you worked in London, how do you think things might be different?

Hypothetical and therefore not relevant

12. Please tick the type of book most children prefer (tick only one) :
    a. a book with pictures   [ ]
    b. a story book   [ ] ← *Categories are not clear – a story book could be a book with pictures*
    c. a factual book   [ ]
    d. a familiar story e.g. the three bears   [ ]
    e. Other; please state ....

Thank you for your co-operation. The next phase of this research involves the interviewing of a sample of respondents. If you do not wish to be further involved, please put a cross in the box above.

↑ *Will respondents read this and locate the box?*

Questions

1   How many faults did you identify?

2   Were there any other things that you noted that aren't given above?

3   How do you think a person would feel about a questionnaire presented such as this? Do you think they would see it as important?

4   How might it affect the responses you get?

Organising a questionnaire

Once you have drafted the questions, you need to ensure you group them in some sort of ordered manner so that, where appropriate, one question leads to another.

One way of doing this is to write the draft questions on small pieces of card or postcards. You can then order and reorder them until you are happy, without having to rewrite the questions every time. It is a better way of assessing the way the questionnaire will finally look rather than just renumbering the questions. Once you are happy with the layout, the questionnaire can be typed up and reproduced as many times as necessary.

Using index cards is one way of organising the order of the questions for a questionnaire

Once you are happy with your questionnaire draft, test it against the checklist of questions below.

Checklist for a questionnaire

◆   Is the questionnaire in a logical order?

◆   Are the instructions on completing the questionnaire clear?

◆   Does it state how to return it?

◆   Are all the questions relevant?

◆   Are personal questions at the end?

◆   Is the language appropriate for the people who are going to complete it?

◆   Are all the questions singular – no double questions?

◆ Do any questions rely too much on memory?

◆ Are any of the questions hypothetical?

◆ Do any questions assume prior knowledge, experience or opinions?

If you still feel the questionnaire is in the format you require, you can now type or write it up.

Should a questionnaire be typed?

There is no rule that questionnaires should be typed, but it does look much more professional if they are. A hand-written questionnaire, no matter how neatly written, does not suggest that the questionnaire is serious and could result in the potential participants not taking it seriously. Using a computer to set up your questionnaire, and to make any changes that are needed, is a considerable advantage. Given that computers are so accessible, there is no reason why a questionnaire should not be typed.

A typed questionnaire will always gain credit for presentation over a written one. Also, if you need to change the questions or the order of layout midway through, you can do this easily on a computer without losing the work you have already done. You can also correct spelling mistakes easily, without using whitener, which can look messy, or crossings out. If hand-written, the whole questionnaire would need to be re-written to deal with all these errors. This would be much more time-consuming.

Piloting the questionnaire

Once you have completed the questionnaire, you need to try it out on other people to identify any areas you have missed. It is always better to have several people looking objectively at the work to comment on it. When you have been working closely on something it is often difficult to see the errors, mistakes or the confusion you have created. The meaning of something may be obvious to you, but to others it may not be.

This process of having other people trial the questionnaire is called a 'pilot'. It is worth piloting the questionnaire on five to ten people, as this will ensure you get a fair view of the quality of the questionnaire.

When you give the questionnaires to the people who are piloting it, ask them to comment on the following points:

How long did it take them to complete it?

Were the instructions clear?

Were any questions unclear?

Were any questions ambiguous?

Did they object to any questions, and if so why?

Had any major areas been missed in the questions?

Was the layout clear?

The results of the pilot questionnaire and the responses to the questions listed above should be analysed. These responses should then be used to adjust the original questionnaire accordingly before it is sent out to the main sample.

It is also important that you write up the findings from the pilot and note the changes made in the work.

Collating and analysing the results

Questionnaires can generate numerical data or large quantities of qualitative information, depending on the types of questions asked. This will influence the way the information is collated and presented.

Questions which generate quantitative or numerical data will usually be presented in a graphical format. Those generating written responses or qualitative information are more likely to be presented in a written form, perhaps classified into groups or summarised under main headings or patterns. Researchers may also use the responses as direct quotes in their write-up.

Results from questionnaires are often initially collated into a results table, as outlined in Chapter 2. From this, they are then presented using graphs and charts. The results table gives an overview of the results obtained and can also start to give ideas about how the data could be presented in a pictorial format. Generally, data from a questionnaire would be converted into graphs, pie charts, pictograms, line graphs or other visual diagrams, as these can highlight the results more effectively than leaving the data in its raw, numerical format. All the different types of graphs are explained in Chapter 2.

The researcher will need to decide which type of graph best presents the information he or she has collected. The advantage in using an Excel package for this is that you can see the information in a range of different formats at the touch of a button. This allows you to make an informed choice without having to spend a lot of time manually drawing different types of graphs.

Try to show a range of different graphs and presentation methods for your questionnaire results, as this demonstrates your skills in data analysis and handling.

Evaluating a questionnaire

When evaluating a questionnaire, you need to consider all aspects of the process, from design to presentation and analysis. You can best evaluate the success of a questionnaire by asking yourself a series of questions. This will help you recognise the limitations of the work.

Was the layout effective?

Was the response rate good?

Was the piloting process effective?

Was your choice of sampling effective?

How did the choice of sample affect the effectiveness of the questionnaire?

How did the piloting process affect the finished questionnaire?

Were the questions clear?

Did the questions get the answers you were looking for?

Did the presentation of the results enhance the work?

How would you change the questionnaire if you were doing it again, and why?

Any evaluative comments should reflect on how the action contributed to the effectiveness of the questionnaire. Always be self-critical in your comments.

Summary

Questionnaires are a really useful way of collecting a lot of information. It can also be done relatively quickly. However, an effective questionnaire has to be carefully thought out to ensure you get the information required. People do not like filling out questionnaires as it takes up their time. They tend to do them as quickly as possible, so it is important to make sure of the following:

The purpose of the questionnaire is clear.

Instructions are clear.

Straightforward language is used.

Only relevant questions are asked.

Questions must be written in a way which all respondents will understand.

Questions must be fair in terms of the demand on memory or experience.

The questionnaire must not be overly long.

Following the guidelines given in this chapter should help you to design an effective questionnaire which meets all these criteria.

ACTIVITY

Study the example of a questionnaire given below.

Playground questionnaire
I am a student in the second year of my AVCE in Health and Social Care. I am studying a unit on early years care. As part of this work, I am doing an investigation into local playgrounds and how they meet the needs of children. I would be grateful if you could spend a few minutes completing this questionnaire.

1   Which is your local playground?
     ....

2   How many children do you have?
     ....

3   What are the ages of your children?
     ....

4   How often do you go to the playground?
     ....

5   What equipment is in the playground?

. . . .

6   Does the equipment meet your children's needs?

. . . .

7   Do you consider the playground to be a safe place to play?

. . . .

8   What other facilities are provided at the playground?

. . . .

9   How would you like to see the playground enclosed?

. . . .

Thank you for taking the time to complete my questionnaire.

Questions

1   Is the preamble sufficient?

2   Identify which questions are open and which ones are closed.

3   Can you identify any potential problems with the way the questions are designed?

4   How could you improve the questions to get better information?

5   What other information would you like to get from this questionnaire?

6   Are the instructions for return clear?

7   What would be the most suitable way of presenting the results?

Further reading

Bell, J (1999) *Planning your research project*, Open University Press, Buckingham
Green, S (2000) *Research methods*, Stanley Thornes, Cheltenham

7 Interviews

In the last chapter, we looked at questionnaires and how to construct these effectively. In this chapter, we will cover interviews and how to get the best from this method of research. Interviews are often used as a research method. This is because a researcher can get a lot of detailed information from a well-constructed interview. However, like questionnaires, there is considerable skill needed in devising good interview questions. You also need to give a lot of thought to the manner in which the interview is carried out, and how it will be recorded. In this chapter, we will cover.

◆ Why are interviews popular as a method of research?

◆ Why are interviews chosen?

◆ Advantages and disadvantages of interviews

◆ Different types of interview

◆ Whom do you interview?

◆ Sampling for interviews

◆ Length of interviews

◆ Presenting interviews

◆ Being objective

◆ Devising and asking interview questions

◆ Recording the interview

◆ Writing up interviews

◆ Analysing the results

◆ Making generalisations from interviews

◆ Evaluating interviews.

Why are interviews popular as a method of research?

Interviews are a popular research method because they provide more detailed information than questionnaires. Interviews take longer to carry out than questionnaires, but they make it possible to explore issues in more depth. In some interviews, it is also possible to respond to the answers the interviewee gives and adapt the questions. This means that an interviewer can get more information from this method.

Interviews have a clear advantage over questionnaires in that they tend to have better response rates. People who are asked questions directly are more likely to answer them, whereas a questionnaire can be easily discarded or forgotten.

Interviews can be tape-recorded which means that researchers can replay an interview as many times as they need to extract the information. However, the interaction between the interviewer and the participant can affect the response. Factors such as the interviewer's appearance, gender, age, and even accent, can affect the answers they get.

It is also easy for interviewers to influence responses without knowing they are doing so. This can be through normal gestures such as nodding or smiling, which are normal habits when talking to people. Uttering 'mmm' or even 'Yes' when someone speaks can influence the relationship.

ACTIVITY

Observe someone talking to another person. This could be a teacher talking to a student, two adults having a conversation, a shopper talking to an assistant, or an interview on television.

Watch how the non-verbal body language helps to keep the conversation flowing.

Why are interviews chosen?

Interviews are a good way of focusing in on an issue in more depth. They allow researchers to collect more detailed information on their chosen topic. As it involves speaking directly to someone, it often means that a researcher can capture more personal views and experiences. Interviews can draw out reasons and explanations in a way that questionnaires cannot. This is because questionnaires are usually designed for limited responses, as this makes them easier to analyse. Also, people often write as little as possible when they are asked to fill out a questionnaire, even when free response is possible.

Advantages and disadvantages of interviews

Advantages

Interviews are based on interaction between two people. If a good rapport develops, the interviewer will have a better chance of getting detailed information. Such a relationship will allow the interviewer to ask questions of a personal and sensitive nature.

Interviews allow people to speak directly and at length in a way that questionnaires do not.

Some types of interview allow interviewers to follow up responses and this makes them more reactive. It allows researchers to get more detailed information.

Questionnaires can be very factual, whereas interviews allow researchers to find out reasons and understand people's thinking.

Disadvantages

The role of the interviewer is very important and the success of the interview may rely on his or her communication skills.

Interviewers can unconsciously affect the responses. Non-verbal communication, such as frowning, smiling or nodding, can influence what an interviewee says or discloses. If they feel the interviewer disapproves of their views, they may not be as open as they could be.

In informal interviews, where the interviewer can follow up responses, it is easy to introduce inconsistency as interviewers may follow up only what they consider to be important.

Interviews are time-consuming and as they are often one to one, they are expensive in terms of time. Therefore, they are generally used for smaller samples.

Interviews gather information about individuals' views, and they can be very different. This can make it more difficult to draw overall conclusions or generalisations. It is not a research method that usually produces detailed statistics.

Interviewees may respond to questions according to what they think the interviewer wants to hear, rather than their true feelings or behaviour.

Different types of interview

There are different approaches in using interviews as a method of research.

Formal or structured interviews

A formal interview is where there is a standard set of questions which are used for each participant. As an interviewer you can ask only these questions, despite the responses given. Interviewers are not able to adapt the wording of the questions, nor change them in any way. It is a very rigid form of interviewing, and is similar to the questionnaire.

It also reduces the chance of bias affecting the interview, where interviewers allow their own views and feelings to influence what they are asking.

Designing the questions for a formal interview follows a process which is very similar to that of designing a questionnaire.

Formal interviews:

◆ use standardised questions which allow generalisations to be made from the results

◆ have less chance of introducing bias by the interviewers as they have to stick rigidly to a set of questions

◆ may lose opportunities for developing information as interviewers cannot follow up answers which may be of interest.

Informal or unstructured interviews

These are interviews where the interviewer has much more control over the questions that are asked. Interviewers usually have a list of areas or issues they wish to cover during the interview. These are often called 'trigger questions'. They are also able to follow up responses and develop the interview more fully. This type of interview can produce richer information as interviewers can probe for thoughts and develop what might appear to be off-the-cuff comments into fuller answers.

The interview process often reflects more of a discussion than a question-and-answer session, and therefore is more unpredictable.

Semi-structured interviews

These interviews are a combination of formal and informal interviews. The interviewer will have a number of questions he or she needs to ask. The rest of the interview will cover a list of areas or issues and the interviewer will be able to follow up points made by the interviewee.

Imagine you are researching attitudes to older people. Devise a list of trigger questions which you could use in an interview situation.

Use the questions to carry out a formal and an informal interview of two different people.

1   Which type of interview gave you the most information?

2   Why do you think that was?

3   How do you think your body language might have influenced the way the interview went?

4   Could the formal interview be developed to get better information?

Whom do you interview?

Whom you choose to interview will depend on your research. As interviews take more time than questionnaires, though the amount of information is greater, you are likely to interview fewer people. Therefore, you need to choose your interviewees very carefully.

If interviewing is the main method of research, you are likely to interview more people. If interviews are being used to support questionnaires, then the number of people interviewed will be less.

The number of people interviewed will need to be enough to be able to draw valid conclusions.

Sometimes you will interview a number of people on the same issue; at other times you may develop a particular interview for a particular person. In this case, you may use your interview only once.

Sampling for interviews

Sampling methods can apply to interviews when you intend to interview more than one person. A sampling frame will need to be developed. 'Sampling frame' is the name given to a plan which identifies the profile of whom you will interview from a cohort. A cohort is all the people who could be interviewed.

A sample frame is needed to make sure that views are taken from a range of people in the cohort.

Look at the example below.

Jane is researching into the quality of the childcare provided by Jinex Incorporated. She needed to get the views of different staff at all levels as to who uses the service. The sample frame looked like this.

	Male PT	Female PT	Male FT	Female FT
Senior managers	0	0	3	2
Middle managers	0	3	4	3
Operatives	0	4	2	4

Types of sample

Random sample

In this sample, respondents are chosen at random, so everyone on the list has an equal chance of being chosen to be interviewed.

Stratified random sample

This sample reflects the structure of the cohort. Depending on what is being researched and where, this may be based on age group, gender, role or job, or other subgroups which exist within the cohort being analysed. Therefore, you need to analyse the potential respondents before you begin and then ensure your sample reflects this.

For example, imagine you were asked by a company to research the need for work-based canteen provision. The company profile is as follows.

Staffing profile	Numbers	Number of males (%)	Number of females (%)	% of total in company
Senior managers	6	4 (67)	2 (33)	7
Middle managers	8	4 (50)	4 (50)	9
Operatives – full-time	30	20 (67)	10 (33)	36
Operatives – part-time	40	6 (15)	34 (85)	48
Totals	84	34 (41)	50 (59)	100

If you were going to interview a 33% sample (28 staff), select your interviewees as follows.

Staff profile	% of sample	No to be interviewed	Number of males	Number of females
Senior managers	7	2	1	1
Middle managers	9	3	1	2
Operatives – full-time	36	10	7	3
Operatives – part-time	48	13	5	8

This is the **sample frame**. By doing this, you can ensure that every group is represented in the appropriate proportions. This sample reflects the structure of the full company. It can then be assumed that any findings could be reflective of all staff. This careful calculation takes time but it is useful in that any results can be seen as representative of the group being investigated.

It becomes even more complicated if you include consideration of ethnic origin or culture, something you feel must be represented in the cohort.

Cluster sample

In this case the researcher chooses a particular group of people to interview who are located in a particular area for a specific reason. An example may be people who attend a particular day centre.

Such a sample is generally chosen because there is a specific reason for doing so, such as work specifically focusing on that area.

In this type of sampling frame, you are likely to interview all of the target group.

Opportunity sample

This sample consists of anyone who passes by a particular point when the research is being carried out. There is no selecting done by the researcher; all those who agree to be interviewed are included in the sample.

Systematic random sample

This is a structured sample where the researchers choose respondents in an organised way. They generally have a list of people, such as an electoral role or a register. They then choose every so many people on the list, e.g. every sixth person.

This method can also be carried out in the street, where a researcher may interview every fifth person on the list, for example.

Self-selected sample

This type of sampling method is one where people volunteer themselves to take part. People volunteer themselves to be interviewed on a particular issue. Sometimes incentives, such as prizes, are offered to encourage people to do this.

This does mean, however, that you will attract a particular type of person, so your results may be affected.

Whichever method you choose for selecting your sample, it is important you identify your reason for choosing the method in your writing up of the research. Most samples will be a balance between the ideal people to be interviewed and those actually interviewed. This will reflect what is practical and available. The choice is likely to be affected by cost, time and resource limitations but as long as this is recognised in the analysis of the results and the evaluation, then it is reasonable.

Length of interviews

There is no ideal length for an interview, but it is important to remember that interviewees are giving up their time to speak to you, so they need to feel it is well spent. It is good practice to indicate how long an interview is likely to take at the start.

It is important that the interviewer feels that all questions are relevant and that the interview is focused. An interview should not appear aimless and without direction as the interviewee is likely to lose patience and interest. This will not help to ensure that you get the developed responses that you want.

Be purposeful and direct. When the interview is finished, draw it to a close.

Presenting interviews

In interviews, the issue of presentation focuses on the interviewer and how he or she asks the questions.

It is important that interviewers look professional and smart and have the material that they need close at hand. Trigger questions should have been prepared before going to the interview. If you are using a tape-recorder, check it is working before the interview.

Turning up to an interview with crumpled clothing and unwashed hair will not encourage people to want to talk to you.

People are more likely to respond to a smart interviewer

Start an interview by explaining who you are and what you are investigating. Be sure to clarify that all responses will be confidential.

Sometimes a formal introduction is necessary, either through someone else or through a written recommendation on official-headed paper. Generally, people are far more cautious about speaking to strangers nowadays.

Be flexible in your availability for interview. Don't expect the interviewee to be available when it suits you. You are more likely to get a successful interview if you can fit in around their commitments. If they have to fit you in at an inconvenient time, then the interview may be short and you may not get the information you need.

When interviewing for research you will need to fit around the interviewee's time, and not to your convenience

Being objective

It is important that interviews are conducted in a professional manner.

To do this, interviewers need to keep their views and opinions to themselves, even if asked by the interviewee, as this will affect the responses they get. This is not always easy, as everyone has his or her own opinions. It is more difficult if your views are strong. It can also be difficult not to react if the interviewee expresses views that you do not agree with.

However, the key to a good interview is to conduct it without showing any feelings, either positive or negative. Negative messages can be sent by actions which suggest to interviewees that you are not listening. This can imply that their response is not valued. Therefore, interviewers have to be very conscious of what they say and the body language they use.

Think about it

Make a list of body movements that might occur during a conversation and which might suggest the expression of certain meanings or opinions. List them under positive and negative.

For example:

Positive	Negative
Nodding	Wandering eye movements

Interviews are interactive, but remember the aim is to get the views of the person being interviewed. Interviewers must remain as neutral as possible in order to get the most objective responses.

Devising and asking interview questions

Writing good questions for interviews is a skill. Questions need to be clear to ensure that the interviewee understands what you are asking, and phrased to ensure you get them to focus on the area of interest. Remember, the way you frame a question may be misinterpreted by the interviewee. You should spend some time making sure your questions are framed clearly and are relevant before carrying out the interview.

There are several points to bear in mind when designing trigger questions. These will help you avoid the potential pitfalls.

1 Relevance

Make sure that the questions are relevant to the subject the interview is based on. Questions on age and occupation are common, but you need to consider if this information is relevant to your study. The rule is, if the question is not relevant to the study, then leave it out.

Interviewees give up their time to be interviewed, and irrelevant questions are likely to make them not take the process seriously.

2 Language

Think carefully about the language you use and the people you are interviewing. Choose straightforward words that people will understand. The advantage with interviews is that you can rephrase the question if you find the person does not understand what is being asked.

3 Open questions vs closed questions

Interviews can use both open and closed questions – each has a value. Interviews tend to use more open questions than questionnaires as they allow the interviewer to collect more detailed information.

Open questions are useful as they allow the interviewee to talk at length about a subject. The questions are designed in a way which allows a free response. For example:

'What do you feel is the most effective way of ensuring all nursing homes deliver good-quality care?'

Such questions will elicit a wide range of responses, but can make analysis more difficult. However, they do give a more personal insight into the respondents' thoughts. This type of question is useful when personal views and opinions are important.

Closed questions make the respondent's responses more limited. They generally have a Yes or No answer, or there are a number of predetermined responses for the respondent to choose from. Interviewers may include these questions if they wish to collect facts, or where it is reasonable to guess the range of possible responses.

EXAMPLE

Do you eat breakfast every day?   Yes/No

They are also useful where there is a need to categorise age or time into sections which are easy to analyse.

EXAMPLE

How often do you attend the baby clinic?

a once per week   [ ]
b once a fortnight   [ ]
c once a month   [ ]
d less than once per month   [ ]

or

Please state which age group you fall into:

<19 [ ]   19–35 [ ]   36–50 [ ]   51–65 [ ]   >65 [ ]

Note: < means less than; > means more than.

Remember that when classifying age groups there shouldn't be any cross-over in the age spans. The groups should be as the example above and not 18, 18–35, 35–50, 50–65, and so on, as those who are 18, 35 or 50 will not know which category to put themselves into.

Closed questions are far easier to analyse and results can be presented effectively as graphs and charts. Such graphical presentation can enhance the work, show trends and clarify the findings for the reader.

If you are going to use pre-selected responses, it is important that you think about these to ensure that they have clear meaning and that they are sufficiently different for the interviewee to be able to make a definite choice.

EXAMPLE

How do you rate the facilities at the gym?	
Poor	[ ]
Average	[ ]
Good	[ ]

Each interviewee will have a different measurement of poor, average and good. It is difficult to make comparisons as one person's 'good' will be another person's 'average'. The statements are not quantifiable enough.

There are other words which should not be used as they too lack clear meaning. These include 'reasonable' and 'adequate'.

EXAMPLE

How do you rate the range of exercise classes?	
Adequate	[ ]
Reasonable	[ ]
Good	[ ]
Poor	[ ]

Again, each individual will have a different interpretation of these terms. There may also be confusion over 'adequate' and 'reasonable' as both tend to say the same thing.

You should also consider arranging the responses in a logical order. It could be suggested that the order should be good, then adequate and finally poor.

It may be better to quantify opinions on the quality of the service in a different way.

EXAMPLE

Are the times of the exercise class	
Too early	[ ]
Too late	[ ]
Suitable	[ ]
How do you find the delivery of the class?	
Well organised, efficient, starts on time	[ ]
Good organisation but sometimes starts late	[ ]
Poor, frequently late starting	[ ]

Coding closed questions

Often closed questions are pre-coded to make analysis easier and quicker. Each potential response is given a code so that it is not necessary to record the answers in full every time an individual responds.

EXAMPLE

Using the start of an interview on food provision at a local hospital

1 Gender

Male [ ] **A**   Female [ ] **B**

2 Time in hospital

   1st [ ] **A**   2nd [ ] **B**   3rd [ ] **C**   4 + [ ] **D**

3 Ward

Worthington	[ ] **A**
Bosworth	[ ] **B**
James	[ ] **C**
Singleton	[ ] **D**

4 How satisfied are you with the choice of menu?

Fully	[ ] **A**
Partly	[ ] **B**
Not at all	[ ] **C**

The codes are then transferred to a summary sheet or table where columns can easily be totalled for analysis.

Respondent	1 Gender		2 Times				3 Ward				4 Satisfied		
	A	B	A	B	C	D	A	B	C	D	A	B	C
1													
2													
3													
4													

It would be beneficial to do this as a database, as this would enable you to manipulate the data during the analysis stage. It would also allow the data to be sorted so you could compare male and female responses or how many were fully satisfied with the menu on offer, according to ward or the times they had been in hospital.

4 Personal information

Interviewees are more likely to complete personal information, such as age or income, if placed in a range rather than having to give exact information. Therefore, closed questions are best for this type of question.

EXAMPLE

> Is your gross income bracket, per annum:
> ≤ £10,000 [   ] £10,001–£20,000 [   ]   £20,001–£30,000 [   ]   £30,001 + [   ]?

Remember, people do not like giving out personal information, so ask only if it is absolutely relevant and necessary for the research. This should also be obvious to the interviewee.

If you do need to ask personal information, it is often suggested that the questions should be put at the end of the interview. This is because it has less effect in putting off interviewees than being at the beginning. If asked at the end of the interview, the interviewee should have relaxed and may be more willing to answer questions on more personal issues. If the respondent chooses not to, then you still have the information from the rest of the interview.

5 Multiple questions

Make sure the questions ask interviewees for only one answer. It is easy to ask a question which is actually more than one question. An example is:

'How popular is smoking amongst your friends, and why do you think they smoke when it can affect their health?'

In such cases, interviewees may answer only the second part of the question, which will reduce the reliability of your results. However, in an interview, the interviewer can repeat the second part of the question. If both parts of the question are important, it is better to break the question into parts **a** and **b** or make them two separate questions.

1 How popular is smoking amongst your friends?

2 Why do you think they smoke when it can affect their health?

Breaking up a question into separate parts will ensure that all aspects are answered.

6 Assumptions

Try to avoid questions that presume something about the opinions or actions of the respondent. This also applies to knowledge and experiences.

A question such as 'How long did you smoke?' assumes all the people you are interviewing have smoked. Likewise, 'Which foreign countries did you visit on your holiday this year?' assumes everyone has holidays abroad.

You need to be sure that every question asks something that the interviewee can reasonably answer.

7 Memory

'Did you enjoy your first day at school?'

Not many people would be able to answer this question honestly. Most people have short memories for detail. Therefore, it is not wise to ask people for information which goes back five or ten years. Most people may be reasonably expected to remember up to one year before with relative accuracy.

However, if your research relies on gaining information about the past, then interviews are a better method that questionnaires for collecting this information. This is because the interviewer can ask questions as memory joggers to help the interviewee remember. Memory joggers can include specific events which people will remember, such as the Queen's Coronation, a family wedding, or the birth of a child.

You can ask a question to see what information is remembered with ease, such as:

'What can you remember about your school days?'

Then follow up with questions which pick up on the information the interviewee has given. This will help him or her to remember more detail.

8 Leading questions

It is easy to devise questions which suggest a preferred response to the interviewee, particularly if the interviewer feels a particular way.

EXAMPLE

> 'Don't you think that it's important that parents do not smoke around their children as they can give them lung cancer?'

This can lead to bias in the answers. Therefore, it is important that you check your questions rigorously for this before you carry out your interview.

As you can see, designing questions for an interview is not a simple process. It takes a lot of skill and thought to get it right. It is very easy to make mistakes.

Organising the interview

Once you have drafted the questions, you need to ensure that you group them in an ordered way so that, where appropriate, one question leads to another.

One way of doing this is to write the draft questions on small pieces of card or postcards. You can then order and reorder them until you are happy, without having to rewrite the questions every time. It is a good way of assessing the way the interview will flow. Once you are happy with the order, the interview can be typed up and reproduced as many times as is necessary.

Once you are happy with your interview draft, test it against the checklist of questions below.

It is important to organise the flow of an interview

Checklist for an interview

◆ Are the questions in a logical order?

◆ Are all the questions relevant?

◆ Are personal questions at the end?

◆ Is the language appropriate for the people who are going to be interviewed?

◆ Are all the questions singular – no double questions?

◆ Do any questions rely too much on memory?

◆ Are any of the questions hypothetical?

◆ Do any questions assume prior knowledge, experience or opinions?

Recording the interview

Interviews can be recorded in two ways: longhand and using a tape-recorder.

Longhand

This involves writing down the responses given. This is likely to be in note form, because it is unlikely that you will be able to get down every word said.

There are ways to make the process easier, such as taking the response down as a mind map or a spider diagram.

For example, the responses to the question: 'What do you think about the health option range in the canteen?' may be arranged in this way:

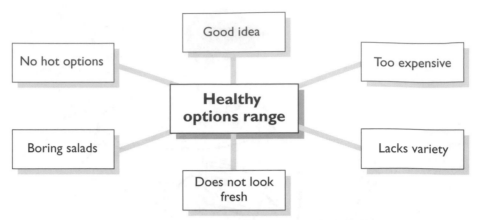

Alternatively, you can develop your own way of writing shorthand by using letters or signs to depict certain words or phrases.

Prearranged headings can also be used where the responses may fall into predictable catagories.

For example:

Healthy food questionnaire: response sheet	
Interview No: M/F	
QI	Cost
	Choice
	Variety
	Appearance
	Taste
	Other

In each case, notes will need to be written up as soon as possible after the interview, before memory fades.

The disadvantage with writing responses longhand, even with the techniques to help speed the process up, is that it can interfere with the flow of the interview. As an interviewer, you will either be concentrating on what is being said and therefore may not get everything down on paper, or you will be so busy writing that you don't hear everything and miss important points which need to be followed up.

ACTIVITY

Ask someone an open question and try to note down the response.

Then feed back to him or her what you have got written down.

How close were you?

Using a tape-recorder

The tape-recorder is a commonly used method of recording an interview. This allows you to compare all the comments made, and to be able to concentrate fully on what the interviewee is saying. The tape can be transcribed at a later date. However, it is worth remembering that a one-hour interview can take 10 hours to transcribe!

The best method is a combination of the two methods: write notes as you go along but tape-record the interview to help you write it up at a later date. It can clarify uncertain points or help the interviewer remember a particular point made.

Writing up interviews

The write-up of the interview should contain all the relevant information, such as the aim of the interview, any sampling methods used, plus a list of the pre-planned questions.

The bulk of the write-up will be the summary of the responses given to the questions.

If a tape has been taken, this can also be included.

Analysing the results

Any closed questions used in the interview should be coded. The best way to analyse these is by using a results analysis table. Using the Excel software package will allow easy analysis and manipulation of the data.

Often, interviews are carried out to give supporting statements to findings from secondary research. Such statements are generally given as quotes. They may be used as follows, for example:

My secondary research suggested that women may feel trapped when they have young children (Oakley 1981). This was supported by the women interviewed.

'...I felt my life was on hold for those few years. They needed 100% of my attention and there was nothing left for me....'

and

'...I felt I had lost my freedom and my identity. I felt angry that I didn't seem to be me anymore....'

Interviews can provide a wealth of material to support information gained through other research methods.

Making generalisations from interviews

Interviews can also be analysed for correlations or generalisations. Drawing hard and fast conclusions should be done with caution, especially if the sample interviewed is small. However, you can still make suggestions based on the evidence you have gained. Make it clear that these generalisations or conclusions are based on a small sample in your write-up and evaluation.

Correlations occur where there is evidence of a relationship between two variables in the data. For example, a series of interviews with new mothers may draw a correlation that those with careers prior to pregnancy are less happy with being full-time mums. However, again you must be cautious with the size of the sample. It is not wise to make the claim that having a career makes women unhappy mothers as there may be other reasons behind such a pattern, which might include the expectations a modern woman has as a result of upbringing and education.

Therefore, outline what your results appear to suggest but nothing more.

Evaluating interviews

It is important that you evaluate your interview in terms of its success and the contribution it made to the overall study.

◆ Reflect on the questions and whether they helped you to gain the information you needed.

◆ Think about how the interviewees reacted to your questioning. Were they at ease? Did you feel they were answering as fully as they could?

◆ Consider the timing and the location of the interviews. Were they suitable and the best for a successful interview?

◆ How effectively did you record and write up the interview?

◆ What would you change if you were doing the interviews again?

ACTIVITY

1   Make a checklist of the important factors when using an interview as a method of research.

2   How can the interviewer try to ensure that bias is not introduced?

3   What characteristics do you consider make a good interviewer?

Further reading

Bell, J (1999) *Planning your research project*, Open University Press, Buckingham
Green, S (2000) *Research methods*, Stanley Thornes, Cheltenham

8 Observations

This chapter looks at another primary research method which can produce a wealth of information. In health and social care, especially early years settings, observations are frequently used as a means of gaining information about the clients carers are working with. Observations can help professionals make decisions about how to work with clients.

In this chapter we will cover:

◆ Why do we use observations?

◆ Ethical issues in observation

◆ Developing a scientific approach

◆ External factors that affect observations

◆ Carrying out an observation

◆ Observing children

◆ Why observe?

◆ Participant versus non-participant observation

◆ Covert or overt observation

◆ Writing up observations

◆ Different types of observation

◆ Evaluating observations.

Why do we use observations?

We use observation to inform our thinking every moment of the day. Our brain translates what we see into meaningful information which we then act upon. Our observations help us to decide what to do next. They give us clues about what is happening around us and how we should react. Thus, we use observation to inform action.

Observations can be used in research as a way of analysing and finding meaning in a range of situations. They are commonly used when working with children as a way of identifying the stages of child development, and where a child might fit in this developmental chain. Being able to carry out effective observations as a child carer shows an understanding of the role a child carer has in developing the young child as well as the skills needed to fulfil this role.

Observations are a way of linking the practice to the theory. Students can show their understanding of the theory in a practical way through the observation. In most cases, observations will not be 'textbook norms', but they will enable you to show expected patterns of behaviour.

Ethical issues in observation

When you are observing, it is important to consider the 'rights' of the person being observed. This means thinking about the need to maintain confidentiality and anonymity for that person. These values are part of the **ethics** of research practice.

Ethics are concerned with human behaviour, whether something is carried out in a morally right or wrong way, and the effects that actions have on others.

> The *Collins Concise Dictionary* (1995) defines ethics as:
> 'The philosophical study of the moral value of human conduct and the rules and principles that ought to govern it.'

Ethical values are used as guidelines when making decisions. Each of us has a set of ethical values which govern what we believe is right and wrong. These may differ from person to person, but in any society they are broadly similar. They are based on the values we are taught as we are brought up and they will influence our behaviour and attitude as well as our conscience.

In carrying out observations, we can say whether the practice is ethically good or bad by the way in which those observations are carried out and how the information gathered is used.

When you carry out an observation, you need to be aware of ethical issues which affect what can be done. Those being observed have a right to the information which is being collected about them. You may need to seek their permission before you can carry out any observations. This may be from the person himself, if he is an adult, or the parent, guardian or carer, if the person is a child.

You must be aware of the principle of confidentiality. All information collected is confidential. It is important that you do not discuss the information you gather with your family or friends. This can happen when you are chatting casually, but you could find yourself in a very difficult situation if you were overheard or if someone repeated your comments.

All observations should show an awareness of culture, race, family circumstance, gender, disability, age and sexual orientation. Respect for others includes respect for their customs and beliefs.

In order to maintain confidentiality, it is important that the participants, that is the people you are observing, remain anonymous. This can be achieved by using letters rather than names.

Photographs or videos

It is often tempting to include photographs or videos of the person being observed as part of the evidence. These can be a way of illuminating an area of study. They should be used only as a way of making the information more explicit or to demonstrate some point. Photographs which just look very pretty or pad out the work should not be used.

Any photograph or video which is used must be commented on or explained. This is a good test of the usefulness of a photograph. If there is nothing to say about it, then it shouldn't be included.

You will also need permission to use photographs either from the parents or guardian if the subject is a child, or from the individual herself if she is an adult.

Health and safety

Adults who work with children have a responsibility to protect them. This means preventing infections as well as accidents. Adults also need to know what to do if a child does have an accident.

This unit will help you understand what causes some infections and also how infection can be spread. You will learn about practical ways of preventing the spread of infection. The unit also looks at ways in which adults can help prevent accidents as well as what you should do if there is an emergency or an accident. The unit covers the following:

- the importance of good personal hygiene
- how to prevent the spread of infection
- how to store and handle food safely
- how to ensure home and group settings are safe and healthy
- basic first-aid principles and actions to take in an emergency.

The development of motor skills

Fine motor skills   **Gross motor skills**

Figure 8.2   The development of motor skills

Age	Gross manipulative skills	Fine manipulative skills
6 months	Can roll from front to back. If held in a standing position, bounces up and down. Can put his or her feet into his or her mouth. Sits with support.	Stretches out with both hands for interesting small objects within grasp. Passes large objects from one hand to the other, occasionally dropping objects.
12 months	Can sit from lying down. Walks with both hands held by another; some may walk alone. Can sit up unsupported. May attempt to climb the stairs.	Has a 'pincer grip' and can pick up tiny objects, such as beads, with finger and thumb. Points well. Drinks from a cup and is starting to feed him or herself. Still turns a spoon upside down to get it into his or her mouth occasionally.
18 months	Walks and runs safely. Can kneel and bend without wobbling. He or she can climb the stairs, but comes down backwards, facing the treads. Pushes toys along.	Scribbles with crayons, pulls off shoes, hats, gloves. Can stack a tower of three cubes. Turns pages well, and is beginning to show a preference for one hand over the other.
2 years	Walks upstairs and downstairs holding the banister. Runs and climbs. He or she can stand on tiptoe, and jump off a low step. Riding wheeled toys is possible.	Can unwrap a sweet. Can help get him or herself dressed and builds towers of more than seven bricks. He or she feeds him or herself well and can draw circles and dots with accuracy.
3 years	Climbs stairs like an adult, but may still come down more cautiously. Throws and kicks a ball strongly; may be able to catch a large ball with two hands. Riding a three-wheeled bike is possible.	Can draw a recognisable, if odd, human form. Builds a high tower and a simple bridge with bricks. Some may use scissors with help
4 years	Climbs ladders, hops and jumps with ease. Can avoid things when running and walk down a line.	Can do simple jigsaw puzzles and shape puzzles. Eats tidily and drinks from a tumbler. Buttons are no longer difficult, although zips may be a problem. Draws well.
6–8 years	Rides a two-wheeled bike, balances and has control of general locomotion. Plays ball games with accuracy. Skips. Can stand on one leg for about ten seconds without wobbling.	Writes and draws neatly. Uses construction toys with ease, can sew, cut and most can tie their shoelaces. Could make a sandwich or cut a slice of cake. Eats neatly (mostly!)

Do the photographs on the pages from health and social care books above add meaning to the text

Developing a scientific approach

When carrying out observations, it is important that you develop a scientific approach to your work. This means that you need to carry out the process in an ordered, systematic way to make sure that what you do is accurate. You need to be objective, which means you observe with an open mind. If you know the person you are observing, it is easy to allow what you already know to affect what you see them doing and how you record it. Knowing someone can reduce the objectivity.

For example, if you were observing a child's language ability by asking him or her to read a set of words, you may find the child gets wrong a word you know he or she has previously got right. In this case, it would be easy to record what you know rather that what you have observed.

This is known as having pre-conceived ideas. You must be totally objective and record only what you have seen. If you do not do this, then the whole observation will be invalid. The findings will not be accurate, and will therefore be meaningless. It is very important that you are objective from the start.

Being objective also means that you do not become personally involved with your subject or subjects. The word 'subject' can be used to describe the person or people you are observing. It can be very easy to become emotionally involved, especially when working with children, and this can affect how objective you are. You need to be able to stand back and write what you see, not what you think you see because you are influenced by other information you already have.

ACTIVITY

Ask someone to carry out an observation with you. You can observe anything: children at play, people holding a conversation, students in the canteen. Carry out the observation for five minutes.

Individually, write down what you see. Do this without discussing the work with each other.

After the five minutes, compare notes.

1   How easy was it to observe?

2   How much did you write? Too much or too little?

3   Did you note down the same things? If not, why not?

4   Have you written down only what you saw without bringing in personal opinion?

5   How would you change your approach if you were doing the observation again?

No two observations are the same. In fact, if you achieve about 80% the same, you are doing well. It can be very easy to introduce opinion or your own thinking rather than writing what you see. Many factors affect what we remember and note down when observing something, including our own experience, issues that are important to us, awareness of what is going on at the time, our own concerns or issues, and things which have happened recently.

Being able to observe someone and pass on information without bias is difficult. In all observations, you must try to be objective and not introduce your own ideas or generalisations. Interpretation enables you to make sense of what you see, and to explain it.

External factors that affect observations

The objectivity of observation can be affected by the actions of the observer. Other factors can also affect the situation and the person being observed, so that he or she behaves in a way which is out of the ordinary. It is worth being aware of some of these factors.

Familiarity with the environment	If the person being observed is in an environment which is familiar to him, then he will be more relaxed and feel more comfortable. The observation which takes place in this situation is likely to depict a more accurate impression than one which takes place in unfamiliar surroundings.
Timing of the observation	Observing a child who is waiting for an appointment and is perhaps anxious, is likely to produce an observation of non-typical behaviour. This is not the sort of situation in which to carry out a straightforward observation. However, it may be that the observation is done to look at how the unknown does affect the behaviour of a child.
Environmental factors (e.g. the weather)	Windy or stormy weather is known to have an effect on behaviour, and so you may get observations that are out of the norm when observing in these conditions.
Times of the year	There are certain times of the year when children get excited, such as Christmas, and this is likely to affect the observation results.
Changes in the immediate environment	Changes in noise levels, changes in the organisation of the immediate environment, or changes in the normal people who are usually in an area, e.g. a supply teacher or new colleague. These can all trigger changes in behaviour which will be reflected in any observation that is carried out.

An observation needs to be a true record which is not adversely affected by anything, as this makes it easier to interpret. It also gives a fairer analysis of what is going on.

Cultural issues

All cultures have their own norms and values. This means that different things are accepted as being normal, so you need to ensure you avoid making value judgements which are linked to culture. Cultural behaviour can be difficult to identify, and it can be easy to make judgements about what you observed based on your own cultural standards. It would be useful to fully investigate the culture before carrying out any interpretation.

For example, Japanese people do not display anger or frustration in their facial expressions. They do not expect others to do this either. They also tend to look at the neck when talking to someone, rather than looking him directly in the face.

Therefore, if you observed a Japanese child interacting with European children, you might see very different emotions displayed during the play session. Knowing about the culture would help you to interpret what you saw far more sensitively.

Another example is staring or gazing. In Northern European and Asian cultures, it is rude to gaze at someone for too long. Children are taught not to do this. However, in Southern Europe, Arabic and Latin American cultures, too little gazing is seen to be rude and impolite. It is also seen as a sign of insincerity.

Some cultures also use gestures more than others. In Britain there are about 20 common gestures such as nodding or shrugging the shoulders. Other cultures, such as that of Italy, have hundreds of gestures which are commonly used in speech.

Our cultural habits are also displayed in the way we greet people. In England, a common way of greeting someone is to shake hands. In European countries, such as France, it is common to see people greeting each other with a kiss. In Arabic or Latin American countries, a kiss or a hug is also a common greeting.

Make sure you always consider cultural behaviour when you try to interpret what you have seen.

Carrying out an observation

In our culture, we are taught that staring is rude and that we shouldn't stare at others. Therefore, most people avoid doing it. Observations, however, require you to do just that, watch someone for a period of time. This can feel uncomfortable especially when observing the first few times. Observations follow strict guidelines and ethics. Also, observations should have a clear purpose and reason, which makes them very different from just looking at someone for the sake of it.

Sometimes when observing in organisations or groups, such as residential care establishments or nurseries, you may observe things that you feel show bad practice. In many cases, this can be seen as a positive criticism for staff involved to consider, and most professionals would take such comments on board. Under the Human Rights Act, those being observed will have the right to see what has been written about them, so bear this in mind when writing the observation. If you follow the guidelines and write only what you see, those being observed cannot argue with you. Make sure you do not interpret it personally in any way, and then you will not be criticised.

It is worth remembering that it is unlikely that you will observe a textbook case when you carry out an observation.

Step-by-step guide to carrying out an observation

To carry out an observation successfully, you need to have an organised approach. It is wise to become familiar with the steps you need to go through to make sure you are well prepared to observe. In most cases, you will plan your observation before you carry it out so there should be no excuse for poor preparation.

1 Decide what you want to observe, and how and when you are going to observe it. Make sure you have all the necessary permissions. You should also have decided on the time you intend to spend on the observation.

2 Gather together the equipment you need for the observations – pen, materials for use during the observation, such as puzzles, tape-recorder, camera or video, if appropriate.

3 Make sure you have all the paperwork you need – checklists, paper.

4 Find an appropriate place to carry out the observation. When carrying out a non-participant observation, make sure you sit where you aren't distracting anyone. When carrying out an observation where you need to interact with the person you are observing, make sure you choose a place where you will not be in the way or regularly disturbed – for example, in the middle of a room where people are pushing past you all the time.

5 Carry out the observation. Take notes carefully. Try not to move unnecessarily or laugh or sigh as this could affect the concentration of the person being observed.

6 After the observation, write it up as soon as possible. This will help ensure you remember as much as possible.

Observing children

When observing children, it is common to look at specific areas of development. The areas of development generally are:

Physical
Gross and fine manipulative skills, control of larger body parts, such as the head, to the development of fine motor skills, such as threading beads.

Cognitive development
The ability to think, learn and reason.

Language development
The ability to communicate, from the very early communication of gurgles and facial expressions to the ability to communicate using complex words and sentence structures.

Emotional development
How a child moves from being fully dependent on the parents to independence.

Social development
The development of relationships with peers and adults and the ability to react appropriately in social situations.

Observations can be used to analyse the stage a child is at in terms of the norms of development. This can then help the adult to decide how to support a child to develop through to the next stage. Observations can also help identify when a child is well outside the norm for its age and stage of development. It may alert you to the need for some specialist help or advice.

Observations can also help you appreciate the different human needs. Maslow developed a hierarchy of human needs.

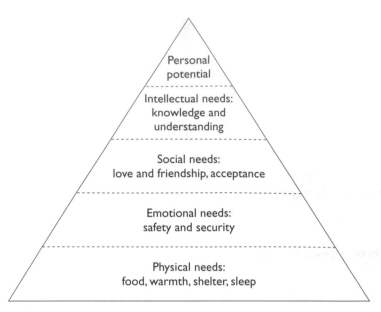

Maslow's hierarchy of human needs

Maslow believed that the lower layers of his triangle have to be satisfied before an individual can move up. Being aware of this theory may help you to understand some of the things you may observe. For example, a child may not be able to concentrate on a task because he has not eaten any breakfast. According to Maslow's theory, his physical needs haven't been satisfied and so he cannot move on to a task which requires him to focus on satisfying a need further up the scale.

ACTIVITY

Can you think of some other examples of how a child's performance may be affected by emotional, social or physical factors.

An awareness of these needs can be important when working with parents. Carrying out observations will make you more aware of these needs and how behaviour can be affected if they are not met. It can also help you to identify when there is a change in behaviour for a certain reason, such as a change in family circumstances or a new baby brother or sister.

Why observe?

We observe for a number of reasons. As we have already discussed, observations are used as a way of understanding child development. They can also be used as a way of looking at social relationships. A researcher may observe people to see how they react in certain situations or to certain stimuli, for example how they respond to advertisements or to waiting in a doctor's surgery.

You might also observe the behavioural pattern of people on a particular type of medication to see how it affects them. Observations can also be used to look at interactions between people in a range of settings, such as residential care or in public places.

Observations can be used to study all aspects of development, including physical, social, emotional and intellectual development. They can be used as the main method of research in a longitudinal study, i.e. a study which takes place over a longer period of time – perhaps six months or more – to chart developments over a period of time. They may also be used as a research method to support others or used as a one-off piece of work.

Examples of different pieces of work or projects where observations may be used include:

1 Child studies

2 Social interaction in residential care

3 Effects of advertising/marketing techniques on purchasing habits

4 Interaction of children in a playgroup setting

5 Language development studies.

Participant versus non-participant observation

Observers can carry out their observations by participating or not participating in what is going on in different ways. They can choose to get involved in the activity or to simply watch what is going on. Either way can affect how the observation develops. So, it is worth considering the best approach for the type of observation you are intending to carry out before you do it.

Participant observation

Participant observations are those in which the observer becomes part of the group being observed or observes someone as she works alongside him. An example is observing a child's fine motor skills while doing a puzzle with him.

This observer is participating with the child in the activity

Participant observation may result in a more reflective picture of what normally goes on as the observer is part of the group. However, being part of the group makes it more difficult to record as many details of what is happening as you may need. You may also influence the outcome by your involvement.

Non-participant observation

In this type of observation observers are onlookers who are outside the action. They have no interaction with the people they are observing. An example is an inspector observing a nursery or a care establishment in operation.

Both types of observation have advantages and disadvantages. When non-participant observation is taking place, the observer may have an effect on the dynamics of what is going on as the people concerned know they are being watched. This situation can appear false, and so you may not get a true picture of what happens as people feel intimidated.

The advantage of this type of approach to the observation is that the observer can compile a lot of detail about what is happening. He or she can see things that participants cannot because they are fully involved.

This observer is not participating in the activity, but simply observing it

Which type of observation do you think is better for the following investigations and why?

◆ An investigation into teenage eating habits.

◆ Observing the concentration span of children over an hour.

◆ Looking at how advertising affects people's purchasing habits.

Covert or overt observation

Observation can be carried out overtly, where the observer does not hide what he is doing, or covertly, where the observer does not inform people what he is doing or why.

Covert observations may raise ethical issues, as those being observed could claim they are being deceived.

What do you think are the advantages and disadvantages of covert versus overt observations?

Identify situations in which each may be beneficial and give reasons for your suggestions.

Writing up observations

Observations need to be written up in a particular way. Using specific headings will help you make sure you record all the necessary information. There are two main sections to an observation:

◆ **The preliminaries** – information that sets the context in which the observation is taking place.

◆ **The body of the observation** – the actual observation itself and the analysis.

The preliminaries

This sets out clearly all the background information on the observation so that the reader knows where it took place. It will also highlight any factors that might affect what has been observed, such as who else is present or anything unusual about the day or time.

The information is broken down into a number of headings:

The aim of the observation or the reason for doing it	You need to explain why you are doing the observation and what you are looking at.
Context or setting	You need to explain where the observation is taking place, e.g. a residential home, a nursery, a shopping centre.
Immediate context	You need to give specific details of the area in which the observation takes place, e.g. if in a residential home, you need to state exactly where, e.g. the lounge.
Numbers of adults/children	You need to outline: ◆ Who is specifically involved in the observation. ◆ Who is close by, in the room or area.
Specific details on the person being observed	You need to give some information about the observee, including: ◆ Coding to identify person being observed (No names, to retain confidentiality) ◆ Age ◆ Gender ◆ Other relevant information, e.g. position in the family if a child, length of time living in a care home if looking at someone in residential care.
Method of observation	You need to specify the type of observation that you have chosen to do, e.g. written record, time sample, etc.
Media used	You need to explain how you are going to record the information, e.g. tape, photographs, written.

Body of the observation

The observation	This is the actual observation itself. You record exactly what you see. You must make sure that you do not include personal opinions at this point. Just write what you observe.
The interpretation	This is where you analyse what you have seen. You can make personal comment and judgement in this section, but make sure your comments are supported with quotes or references from theorists or textbooks. This ensures that your comments are valid and carry credibility.
Recommendations	Some observations require you to make recommendations. This is likely to be relevant if you are observing someone in relation to his or her level of skill, learning or social ability. A recommendation may need to be made which suggests what could be done next to help develop that aspect of the person.
Bibliography	You must produce a bibliography which states all the sources of information you have used to write up the observation.

Finding quotes or references to support observations can be one of the most difficult aspects of doing an observation. One tip to make this easier is to use the index in textbooks to find appropriate quotes on the topic you are observing. Make sure you note down the information needed for the bibliography when you do this.

Once you have a list of possible quotes, you can pick appropriate ones to support the findings of your observation.

You may need to look for specific quotes once you have carried out the observation, but you should find that you have something that will help you get started.

ACTIVITY

Using the topic of non-verbal communication, look in some textbooks for quotes related to the topic.

Carry out a five-minute observation of two people talking, noting down the body language that is used.

Look at your chosen quotes. Try to apply them to what you have seen.

Different types of observation

There are a number of different types of observation which can be used according to what you are looking at. The table on pages 142–144 outlines the main types of observation and their strengths and weaknesses.

Evaluating observations

After carrying out observations as a research method, it is important to evaluate them in terms of how effective they were as a method of gaining information to inform the work. Therefore you need to analyse in terms of:

- How effective was the choice of observation?
- Did it meet the original aims which you set out to achieve?
- Was the observation well planned?
- Were any check sheets or materials required prepared in advance?
- Did you get all the permissions required?
- How well did the observation fit in with the routine that was going on at the time?
- Was the process of observing affected in any way? If so, how did this affect the observation?
- Did the process of observation affect what the person being observed was doing? Do you think it made him or her act in an unusual way? If so, how did this affect the observation?
- Did the observation manage to get all the information required?
- Would you change the type of observation you chose to do? If so, why? If not, why not?
- Did you record the evaluation effectively?
- Did you manage to get all the information required?
- Was the observation written up in an effective manner?
- Did you link your observation effectively to theorists?
- Were you able to make effective and realistic recommendations?

When you are evaluating, aim to analyse the whole of the observation process and reflect on how effective the whole process has been.

Table 8.1   Main types of observation and their strengths and weaknesses

Type of observation	How to use this type of observation	Example of how it may be used	Advantages of this type of observation	Disadvantages of this type of observation
Time sample	◆ When recording activity over a long period of time, e.g. every five minutes to record what a child is doing ◆ Often used if there is concern as it can help establish if the problem is real ◆ Best carried out over a number of days	◆ How a child fills his time ◆ To see if a child is joining in activities with other children ◆ To assess concentration spans ◆ To see how often a piece of equipment is used	◆ Produces detailed information and gives a clear picture of what is happening ◆ Child may be absent after the first day and so pattern of observation may be broken	◆ Time-consuming exercise ◆ Interrupts the natural flow of work as someone has to stop regularly to do the observation

Event sample	◆ Used when recording how often a particular 'event' happens. This may include unsocial behaviour such as biting, kicking or tantrums
	◆ Can also look at factors which might be provoking certain actions, including what happens immediately before the event takes place
	◆ Could be used to note issues of concern or changes that have been observed, such as loss of concentration
		◆ To look at how often a particular event happens such as:
		  – Biting
		  – Swearing
		  – Spitting
		  – Kicking
		  – Hitting
			◆ Produces detailed information on the behaviour of a particular child
			◆ Will clearly show if there is a need for concern
			◆ Will clearly show if something is triggering the action
			◆ Information can be easily understood by all involved
				◆ Need to keep focused on one particular child for a long period of time
				◆ Can interrupt the natural flow of the activities of the day
				◆ Child may sense she is being watched and this may trigger behaviour which is not usual for that child

Free response or written record	◆ Used to record what you see over a set period of time ◆ Often used for 'spur of the moment' observations	◆ To observe a naturally occurring event	◆ Can take place spontaneously ◆ Do not need any prepared charts	◆ Longhand exercise ◆ Can be off-putting to those being observed – it is not always easy to be inconspicuous

Method	Description	Uses	Advantages	Disadvantages
				◆ Can be difficult to write down and watch at the same time – may miss things as they happen
Target child	◆ A method used to observe one particular child over a long period of time ◆ Records the activities of a child, as well as how he reacts with others and the language they are using ◆ Coding is often used to help record all that is seen	◆ To observe a child who appears to be withdrawn and is not reacting well to others ◆ To observe how a new child is settling into the group	◆ Detailed focus on one child is very informative ◆ Produces a clear and detailed picture of what is happening	◆ One person is taken out of the regular activities to do this ◆ Poor coding can reduce the accuracy of the overall observation
Checklist	◆ A list of skills or attributes you are looking for or assessing during an observation ◆ Can use to assess one child against the norms for her age and stage of development ◆ Can use to compare skills within an age group or across different ages	◆ Physical development ◆ Gross motor skills ◆ Fine motor skills ◆ Social skills ◆ Reading ability	◆ Quick to carry out ◆ Clear results which can be easily understood ◆ Can make the observation process into a game to make the person being observed less self-conscious	◆ Need to prepare the checklist well beforehand ◆ May not get true results if the person being observed is unco-operative or they feel under pressure to perform ◆ Care is need to be fully objective and only record what you see
Language tapes	◆ When looking at language development the most effective type of observation is to use a tape-recorder ◆ When using a tape-recorder with children, try using a children's tape-recorder, as this will not seem so out of place and can record as well as an adult one	◆ Language such as: – Circle time – Stories – Language used when playing a game – Language used during pretend play, such as the home corner	◆ Do not need to write everything down ◆ All language is recorded and nothing is missed	◆ Takes a long time to transcribe tapes ◆ A tape-recorder may put the children off

Table 8.1 (continued)

Type of observation	How to use this type of observation	Example of how it may be used	Advantages of this type of observation	Disadvantages of this type of observation
	◆ Make sure you identify who and what is being recorded at the start of the tape			
Sociogram	◆ Used as a way of looking at social interaction and friendship groups ◆ Common method is to ask children to name or draw their three best friends. This is plotted against all the children in the group to assess popularity ◆ Can also look at gender differences in friendship groups or friendships grouped according to ability in the setting	◆ Social relationships Friends named by Teresa: Jane Jane: Abi, George Abigail: Emily, Amber James: George: Abi, Emily Ben: Emily: Abi	◆ Can develop the observation into an activity ◆ Fairly quick to do ◆ Can help to identify children who may need help or support to be part of the group	
Movement chart or flow chart	◆ This is a good way of looking at how children use a piece of equipment over a period of time and how popular it is ◆ A way to note how long a child spends on any one activity	◆ Observing the: – Use of toys – Attention span of a child – Popularity of a toy – Activity of a child over a period of time	◆ The information has limited use – may be helpful in deciding what type of toys to spend more money on ◆ Can be used to see how a toy might be developed to hold the attention span longer	◆ Does not provide a wealth of information
Assessing cognitive development	◆ Tests based on Piaget's work with children can assess levels of understanding ◆ Used with children up to 8–9 years	◆ Piaget believed that children of 5–6 years cannot conserve. This means that their opinions about the size and weight of things are affected by physical appearance. They cannot understand that the volume or weight of something can stay the same even if the shape changes	◆ Allows development to be linked to a cognitive stage ◆ Allows comparison across and within age groups	◆ Children might not perform well under pressure

ACTIVITY

Think about the following senarios. For each one, suggest:

◆ The type of observation that could be carried out.

◆ If the observation should be participant or non-participant.

◆ How the observation should be recorded.

I Salim is looking at the interaction between clients in a day care centre for the elderly. He wants to identify ways in which communication could be improved.

2 Jane is investigating school playground games. She wants to see if they have changed in the past 50 years.

3 Mark is looking at the development of children's drawing. He wants to look at the stages of development up to six years old.

4 Ali wants to study the social skills of a group of special needs teenagers. He has chosen to do this at a mealtime.

Further reading

Bartholomew, L and Bruce, T (1993) *Getting to know you: a guide to record keeping in early childhood education and care*, Hodder and Stoughton, London

Bee, H (1992) *The developing child*, HarperCollins, New York

Bentzen, W (1993) *A guide to observing and recording behaviour*, Delmar, New York

Green, S (2000) *Research methods*, Stanley Thornes, Cheltenham

Hobart, C and Frankel, J (1999) *A practical guide to child observation*, Stanley Thornes, Cheltenham

Tassoni, P and Beith, K (1999) *Nursery nursing: a guide to work in early years*, Heinemann, Oxford

9 Using secondary sources for primary research

In Chapter 3 we looked at how to do a literature search to get secondary information to support an investigation. In this chapter we look at how we can use secondary sources as a primary research method.

There are situations when it is useful to analyse secondary sources, and in such cases, it becomes a primary research method because you are using the material to find out first-hand information. Therefore, this chapter covers:

◆ Using books for primary research

◆ Designing and carrying out a book analysis

◆ Scale and scope of a book analysis

◆ Using promotional material for primary research

◆ Carrying out a gobbledygook test

◆ Presenting and concluding the results from book and leaflet analysis

◆ Evaluating the research method.

Using books for primary research

Books can be used as a primary research method. This occurs when the books themselves are the source of the research and are analysed. An example is analysing the representation of different cultures in children's storybooks.

Designing and carrying out a book analysis

Analysing books is an organised way of identifying specific issues or activities that appear in the texts. It can be qualitative research in that it can analyse an issue in depth or it can be used as a quantitative research method to record details of a specific issue as it is portrayed through books, in terms of how often, how many or how much. How to analyse is a decision which needs to be made with care.

How to analyse books

It is important that any approach should be well thought through, and carried out carefully in an ordered manner. The areas of analysis are pre-chosen by the researchers depending on the issue they are looking at. They will also need to decide if they are looking at a cross-section of texts or focusing in depth on one or two. Once this has been decided, it is essential that the same criteria be applied consistently throughout the analysis. Any change applied midway through will make the results unreliable and have less meaning.

Therefore, it is essential that the categories of the analysis are decided upon at the start of the exercise and not changed. In order to do this effectively, time will need to be spent deciding on the categories. It is then essential that the categories be trialled on at least one source being analysed. This will:

◆ ensure all the appropriate criteria have been covered

◆ ensure you are clear about what your criteria actually cover – a detailed written explanation should be kept

◆ allow expansion of the criteria or the discarding of inappropriate categories before carrying out the major exercise.

An example of an analysis sheet for images of gender roles in children's books is given below.

Portrayal of gender roles in children's books

Book:

The gender for which role applies	The activities being undertaken	Main tasks	Skills being demonstrated
Female adults only			
Male adults only			
Male and female adults			

The complexity of the chart will depend on the issue being analysed.

ACTIVITY

Choose a popular children's book and try out the analysis.
How well does it work?
What conclusions could you draw from this exercise?
What changes would you like to see in the categories?

Scale and scope of a book analysis

You may be faced with a wealth of written material which you have to analyse for your research project. This may be too much to deal with, making the task too huge and cumbersome to be able to complete.

You will then have to take into account how much time you have to complete the research. This may mean that you have to limit the scope of the work to reduce the amount of material that you have to deal with. This can be done in a number of ways, while keeping the required focus.

1 Limit the number of sources by taking representative samples. For example, you could look at the books that are currently in the top ten book list for children. This can be found in bookshops.

2 Limit the time span of the research. Decide to look at books published within a specific time span – obviously the smaller the time frame, the less material you will need to analyse.

3 Limit by the age group that the books are suitable for. This will narrow the focus somewhat, but the ability to limit by this method will depend on the focus of the analysis.

You may need to narrow the scope still further. Whichever way you chose to limit your scope for analysis, it is important that you can justify your actions in terms of the research being carried out. An arbitrary decision about choice of material without justification has the potential to make the research invalid.

When limiting the range of sources, you need to ensure that you do not make sweeping statements in your conclusions. You cannot claim that all books are discriminatory, for example, if you have analysed only one or two texts. Your choice of language will be important. You can state what you have found:

'From my research, it appears that the some books still portray discriminatory messages.'

However, you must recognise the limitations of your work and how this may distort your conclusions.

Using promotional material for primary research

Promotional material, such as leaflets, brochures, prospectuses, political party leaflets, information leaflets from companies on their products, could be used as a primary research method. To do this, the material is analysed in some detail according to the area of study. One example is to analyse a number of leaflets on the same topic to see how the information is presented by the different leaflets. It could also be analysed in terms of how gender roles are presented or how different cultural images are used.

For example, if you are investigating breast or bottle feeding, you can get a lot of promotional material from the Health Education Authority, as well as from bottled milk manufacturers. See the examples opposite.

You could choose to analyse how the companies depict the role of fathers in this process. In this case, you could see if they show a father as being fully involved or if the images and text still present infant feeding as a female role.

You could also look at the images of bringing up children that these leaflets portray. Do the leaflets show happy children with relaxed parents or do they

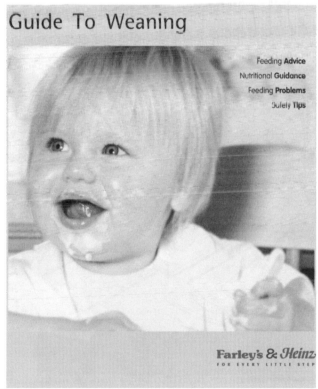

Examples of promotional material

recognise that bringing up children can be challenging. Trying to make children perfectly presented all the time is unrealistic and many parents find child-rearing a tiring process. Is this recognised?

This method could be used to support information that you might have gained through other primary research methods. This is known as **triangulation**, where you use one method of research to support another. This means that you can validate your findings.

An example of using one method of research to support what has been discovered through using another method

When analysing a number of leaflets, it is important to decide on the criteria that you will use, to make sure they are applied consistently across the promotional material.

Collect a range of leaflets on a topic of your choice. This may be on:

◆ *Healthy eating from different supermarkets.*

◆ *Safety information from services such as the fire service.*

◆ *A health issue such as infant feeding, immunisation, a childhood illness, flu injections.*

◆ *Information on sexual health.*

◆ *Information on services of local help groups which may be available from the library.*

Make a list of the different ways in which you might analyse the leaflets.

Develop one idea and carry out the analysis.

What conclusions might you draw?

Example of a leaflet analysis:

Topic: Healthy Eating		
Characteristic	**Leaflet 1**	**Leaflet 2**
Source	Supermarket	Health Education Authority
Type of leaflet	Information and promotion	Information
Front cover	Plain colour with supermarket's own healthy eating symbol	White with colourful pictures of healthy foods
Number of pages/size	4 pages, A5 size	10 pages, A5 size
Target audience	General public	General public
Topics covered	Gives the four areas of healthy eating – low salt, sugar and fat, and high fibre. Brief overview of each and how to improve the diet. Examples given of supermarket's own goods.	Covers each of the four areas of healthy eating in some depth. Explains the effects of eating diets which are high in salt, sugar and fat, and low in fibre. Gives practical ideas on how to adjust the diet.
Language used	Simple language No technical terminology	Some technical words used to explain physical effects of an unhealthy diet. Generally, clear straightforward language.
Percentage of writing compared with images	40% writing, 60% images	80% writing, 20% images
Use of images	A lot of images and pictures used to illustrate the leaflet.	Images and pictures used to support the text.
General comment	Very readable leaflet which the general public would probably look at as it appears accessible and a quick read.	Leaflet contains a lot of valuable information. It is full of facts. It looks wordy and therefore may put some people off.

You could also carry out a gobbledygook test (see below) as part of the analysis and include it in the language-used section. This would help you to identify the type of market each leaflet is aiming at.

You can follow up a leaflet analysis with a survey in which you ask people if they have seen the leaflets before and if they would read them. This would help you to establish how far the appearance and amount of writing in a leaflet affects whether people will choose to read it.

Carrying out a gobbledygook test

It would also be interesting to carry out an assessment of the difficulty of the language. This gives an indication of the readability of the materials. It is based on the assumption that long words and sentences are more difficult to understand.

This can be done by using a gobbledygook test as outlined in Ewles and Simnett (1992).

The test is based on R. Gunnings' Frequency of Gobbledygook formula which attempts to assess the level of difficulty of writing. The system has been adopted by the Plain English Campaign which promotes the importance of using clear English in all communications rather than using complicated and difficult words which only a small well-educated section of the community can understand.

How to carry out a gobbledygook test

1 Choose the piece of writing you wish to analyse and pick a section in the piece which is typical of that writing.

2 Count 100 words of that section and mark it lightly with a pencil (this can be rubbed out afterwards).

3 Count the number of complete sentences in the 100-word sample.

4 Count the number of words in the complete sentences and note them down.

5 Divide the number of words by the number of sentences. This will give you the average sentence length.

6 Read the 100 words through to yourself and count the number of words with three or more syllables. This means a word which is made up of three or more sounds. For example, 'display' has two syllables – 'dis' and 'play'. Dinosaur has three syllables – 'din' and 'o' and 'saur', as does sausages ('saus' + 'a' + 'ges').
The number of words with three or more syllables will give you the percentage of long words in the sample.
Note: Numbers and symbols count as short words, hyphenated words count as two words.

7 Add the number of long words to the average sentence length to give the total score for the sample. The higher the score, the lower the readability.

To make this test fair, you should repeat the exercise at different points in the piece of writing; for example, the beginning, middle and end. There should be at least three samples per piece of writing.

Each score should then be added together and divided by the number of samples taken to get the average score for the piece of writing.

It is then interesting to match scores against the scores of common daily newspapers. This gives an idea of the academic level of the writing and therefore the type of person it is being aimed at.

A test carried out in May 2001 gave the following publications the scores below:

◆ *The Independent*   38

◆ *The Mirror*   21

◆ *The Mail*   24

◆ *Now* magazine   25

◆ *Woman* magazine   21

Carry out the gobbledygook test on the following pieces of writing.

Sample I

Teams are considered to promote a strong learning environment where ideas can be discussed, tested, amended and analysed against the needs of the organisation. Liswood (1990) suggests the needs of an organisation can really develop and move forward if the team is effective. This occurs when the team activity is based on the needs of the team, the individuals within the team and the organisation.

Teams have their own objectives, procedures and approaches to aspects of work but this should reflect the aims of the organisation. They are in a position to examine issues more effectively and from a more balanced perspective than individuals.

Sample 2

Jane looked up at the sky. It was blue with very few clouds to be seen. She heard a noise behind her. It made her jump. She turned around and saw a car had pulled up outside the house. It was her aunt and uncle who had just returned from their holiday. She ran across the field to meet them but she wasn't looking where she was going. She fell over a piece of broken branch and hit the ground with a thump. She lay on the ground for a moment whilst she caught her breath. She could feel a pain in her knee. She looked down and saw bright red blood pouring from a cut.

Presenting and concluding results from book and leaflet analysis

Book and leaflet analyses take specific aspects or issues and look at them out of the context of the text in which they have been written. In doing this, some of the detail and meaning will be lost as it is a broad analysis rather than a specific one. This will need to be recognised when you conclude your results and evaluate the work.

Presenting results

Tables are generally a most effective way to present the results. A table allows the reader to see clearly the full results of the analysis that has been carried out.

It will also be necessary to draw conclusions from your results, trying to make sense of what you have found out through the analysis. If possible, you should then compare your results with other research of a similar nature, or to theories that you have discovered. This will allow you to conclude if your findings are similar to or very different from any work that has gone before.

It will be important to remember that your piece of research is likely to be on a smaller scale than other published material, and this should be reflected in any comments.

Evaluating the research method

The evaluation should show that you recognise the strengths and weaknesses of your work and that you appreciate the effect they may have had on your findings.

In the evaluation, you should look critically at your choice of texts or material, assessing the extent to which it is representative of the range available. You should also evaluate the categories you have chosen to analyse the material, and the extent to which they analysed what you set out to do. Identify any difficulties that arose during the categorisation exercise and state how these may have affected the results, or explain how you dealt with the issue to ensure reliability was maintained.

It will be important to recognise any changes you would make to the approach used, and discuss the potential value such changes would have had for the finished piece of work. Most evaluations identify how the piece of work could be developed.

ACTIVITY

Study the extract from the leaflet below on diet in pregnancy.

While you are
pregnant

While you are pregnant it is important to make sure that you and your unborn baby stay healthy. This booklet gives you information on simple precautions you can take to avoid infections from food and animals. This includes advice on foods which it would be wise not to eat during your pregnancy.

To help you further, there is a checklist at the end of each section of this booklet with tips on general food safety and on safe contact with pets.

A healthy diet is also important when you are pregnant. You can get advice on nutrition from your doctor, midwife, health visitor and from the Health Education Authority's "New Pregnancy Book". Separate advice is available on infant nutrition in the Health Education Authority's 'Birth to Five' book.

Don't become over-anxious about the possibility of catching the diseases described in this booklet. Most of them are very rare, and it is unlikely that you or your unborn baby will be affected. Nevertheless, it is sensible to take the simple precautions given in this booklet to reduce the risk to yourself and your baby.

Food

This section gives advice on the preparation, cooking and eating of some everyday foods. It also tells you which foods you should not eat.

Cheese

You can enjoy hard cheeses such as cheddar. Cottage cheese, processed cheese and cheese spreads, can all be eaten safely as well.

However, while you are pregnant it is wise to avoid all soft ripened cheeses such as Camembert, Brie and similar blue-veined varieties. In the past, some samples of these cheeses have contained high levels of Listeria bacteria, which may harm your unborn child (see page 9).

Sometimes it's not easy to tell the type of cheese, so it is best to check the label. If you're not sure, play safe and don't eat it.

Pâté

Some types of pâté may contain high levels of Listeria. To be on the safe side, do not eat **any** type of pâté while you are pregnant.

Always wash your hands before and after preparing food

Cooked-chilled meals and ready-to-eat poultry

Cooked-chilled meals are ready-cooked foods sold chilled (not frozen) for the customer to eat either cold or reheated at home. Listeria have been found in cooked-chilled meals and ready-to-eat poultry including plain roast chicken. To be on the safe side, you should reheat these types of food thoroughly until they are piping hot throughout rather than eat them cold or lukewarm.

Eggs

Eggs may contain Salmonella bacteria which cause sickness and diarrhoea. While you are pregnant, you should eat only eggs which are cooked until both the white and the yolk are solid. Raw eggs, or foods containing them (such as mousses and 'home-made' mayonnaise) should always be avoided.

Commercially produced products, such as bottled mayonnaise, are made with pasteurised eggs. These may be eaten safely.

Some shops sell pasteurised egg products – either in liquid or dry form – for use at home. These can be used safely in recipes that would otherwise require the use of raw or partially cooked eggs. Once opened or made-up, these products should be treated as fresh egg and used straight away or stored in a refrigerator until needed.

Preparing and cooking poultry, meat and meat products

Uncooked poultry and meat may be contaminated with bacteria which cause food poisoning. These bacteria are destroyed when you cook food at high temperatures, because heat kills bacteria. Raw meat may also contain Toxoplasma, an organism which can, in rare cases, affect the unborn child. Again, this is destroyed by thorough cooking.

Thoroughly wash your hands, and all work surfaces which have been in contact with raw meat and poultry, after handling and preparation. Remember to cook all poultry and meat, including burgers and sausages, so that the juices run clear and there is no remaining blood or pinkness.

Checklist

- Food preparation... Always wash your hands before and after preparing food, especially after touching raw meat, raw poultry, shell eggs and soil covered vegetables and salad stuffs.

- Use one board for preparing raw meat and poultry, and a separate one for other foods. Wash boards, knives, and your hands carefully between preparation stages.

- Take care during the preparation of a meal so that raw food does not contaminate other foods in the kitchen. Take special care when handling meat and poultry that has not yet been cooked.

- Store raw and cooked foods well away from each other – keep any raw meat and poultry on the bottom shelf of your fridge, in a covered container. This is to prevent their juices from dripping on to cooked foods

and especially food that will not be heated before eating including the contents of salad drawers in the fridge.

- Make sure you cook meat and poultry until they are well-done all the way

through to make sure all organisms are destroyed.

- When reheating food, make sure you heat it until it is piping hot all the way through.

Milk

Do not drink raw milk from cows, sheep or goats. This milk has not been heat-treated and may contain bacteria and other organisms which can cause illness. You should avoid these risks by drinking only pasteurised, sterilised or UHT (ultra-heat treated) milk.

Raw cows' milk carries the following warning: 'This milk has not been heat-treated and may therefore contain organisms harmful to health'. This warning has now been extended to raw sheep and goats' milk.

Vegetables and salads

Always wash these carefully to remove any soil and dirt which can carry bacteria and other organisms, making sure that any soil is washed from hands and surfaces also.

Shellfish

When you are pregnant, it is advisable not to eat oysters and other shelled seafoods, such as prawns, mussels and crabs, unless they are part of a hot meal and have been thoroughly cooked. When raw these foods may be contaminated with harmful bacteria and viruses.

Eating out

When eating out either privately or at a party, a barbecue, restaurant or pub, make sure that any meat and poultry you eat is thoroughly cooked right through and served piping hot.

Checklist

● Don't eat raw or lightly cooked eggs, and don't use them in recipes when no cooking is involved – use pasteurised or dried eggs instead.

● Don't eat food which has passed the manufacturers 'use by' date indicated on the label.

Make sure that any meat and poultry you eat is thoroughly cooked right through and piping hot.

Questions

1   What would you consider to be the type of information a pregnant women needs to know about her diet?

2   How effective is the leaflet in terms of

◆ the information provided

◆ the language used

◆ meeting the needs of the target audience

◆ the use of image and colour

◆ the overall layout.

3   Do you feel that the leaflet could be improved in any way? If so, how?

Further reading

Ewles, L and Simnett, I (1992) *Promoting health*, Scutari Press, London

Green, S (2000) *Research methods*, Stanley Thornes, Cheltenham

10 Data collection surveys

As we have already explored in earlier chapters, two of the most popular methods of primary research are the questionnaire and the interview. Both questionnaires and interviews come under the broad umbrella term of 'surveys'.

In this chapter we look at data collection surveys, which are another popular primary research method. Data collection surveys offer another fairly quick way of collecting primary information, but, like questionnaires and interviews, they need to be well planned in order to get the information required. In this chapter we look at:

◆ What are data collection surveys?

◆ Data collection surveys which involve asking questions

◆ Designing data collection surveys

◆ Sampling for a data collection survey

◆ Writing the preamble for a data collection survey

◆ Writing data collection survey questions

◆ Piloting a data collection survey

◆ Data collection surveys which record information

◆ Collating the results from a data collection survey

◆ Evaluating a data collection survey.

What are data collection surveys?

Data collection surveys are used to collect information in a detailed or general way. They are a quantitative research method in that they have the potential to produce a lot of data which is often in a numerical format.

Data collection surveys may take two formats:

1 A list of questions which are asked of people.

2 A chart to record relevant information.

Data collection surveys which involve asking questions

Surveys can be similar to questionnaires in that they collect primary data in a quantitative format. They may consist of a list of questions which the researcher asks people; their responses are then recorded on a sheet. The respondents are not required to complete any paperwork themselves. These surveys tend to be quite short and brief, as people are not keen to spend much time answering questions.

An example of a survey is given overleaf.

*A **data survey** is carried out by asking people questions and recording their responses on a specially designed sheet*

A survey to find out how far people travel to a recycling centre

1   Is this your usual recycling centre?

    Yes   III

    No   I

2   Have you made the trip to the recycling centre especially, or are you combining it with something else?

    Special trip: I

    Combined trip: III

3   If combined, what is it combined with?

    Shopping: II

    Visiting friends   I

    Trip to doctors, dentists, opticians, etc.

    Other, please state: work I

4   How far have you driven to this centre?

    Under 1 mile: II

    1–2 miles   I

    2–4 miles

    4–6 miles   I

    6 miles plus:

With this type of survey, many of the guidelines for formulating questions which apply to questionnaires should also be followed. Before they start the survey researchers should think about what they want to find out and the types of questions that will achieve this. This is particularly important as people tend to be reluctant to spend much time answering questions. A good survey will be short and to the point, with the questions drawing out the required information in a direct way.

Designing data collection surveys

There are two points to consider as you design the survey:

◆ Keep the survey brief – it is important that you bear in mind the length of the survey as you design it. Long surveys will put off potential respondents, who will be less likely to want to answer your questions. Keep it brief; ask only what really needs to be asked.

◆ Have the responses recording boxes on the right-hand side of the sheet, as most people are right-handed The right side allows the researcher to follow the eye and note down responses quickly.

It is important that you are clear from the start what information you want the survey to collect. Having a clear focus will ensure that you find out information that will be of genuine use in your research.

To do this effectively, you should research your topic well. An effective survey comes from thorough research or analysis of other primary research findings. This will give you a good foundation on which to build your survey. The research should help direct you towards what you hope to find out, and will also give you something to compare your results with when you analyse them.

Sometimes the area you wish to investigate has no previously published material available. In this case, you will have to consider your line of enquiry even more carefully to ensure you are clear about the purpose of the survey.

Sampling for a data collection survey

To ensure your data collection survey is valid and reliable, it is important that you consider the people you will ask and how many you will ask. This decision is called your sample. A sample for a survey of this kind is generally affected by the survey having to be carried out in a public place, without access to statistics which might shape the sample. Who you ask will still vary according to the aim of the survey within the scope of the overall research.

The most likely types of sampling method are:

Quota sample

This type of sampling is where you choose the number of respondents you want from each category before the start. You then carry out the survey at random until you have covered the stated number.

Cluster sample

This is a type of sampling where the researcher surveys a particular group of people who are located in a particular area for a specific reason. An example is parents who use a particular playgroup.

Such a sample is generally chosen because there is a specific reason for doing so, such as work specifically focusing on that area.

In this type of sampling frame, you are likely to survey all of the target group.

Opportunity sample

This sample consists of anyone who passes by a particular public point where the research is being carried out. There is no selecting done by the researcher; all who happen to pass by are asked to take part in the survey and included in the sample.

Whichever method you choose to select your sample, it is important you identify your reason for choosing the method in your writing up of the survey. Most samples will be a balance between the ideal sample and what is practical and available. The choice is likely to be affected by cost, time and resource limitations, but as long as this is recognised in the analysis of the results and the evaluation, then it is reasonable.

Writing the preamble for a data collection survey

It is important that you explain the purpose of the survey at the start. This ensures that the respondent is aware of what you are trying to do and why. This can also encourage potential respondents as they can see there is a use or value in doing the survey. You should also assure them of complete confidentiality, as this will encourage more people to be involved.

You should explain how long it will take to carry out the survey as this, again, may encourage more people to take part.

It is also usual to explain how the results will be used.

> **Example of preamble**
>
> I am conducting a survey into how often you visit the dentist, as part of my AVCE in Health and Social Care. All responses are treated in confidence and your name is not necessary. The questions should take about five minutes to complete. The information that I gather will be written up in my research project.

Writing data collection survey questions

Writing good questions for surveys is difficult. They need to be clear to ensure that the respondents understand what you are asking, and also phrased to ensure you get them to focus on the area of interest. It is easy to write a question you think will cover the area you want information about, but those answering the survey may interpret it in a completely different way. Therefore, it is worth spending some time considering your questions to ensure they are right before carrying out the survey.

There are several points to bear in mind. These will help you avoid the potential pitfalls.

1 Relevance

Make sure what you ask is relevant to the survey. Questions on age, gender and occupation are common in surveys, but you need to decide whether this information is relevant to your study. The rule is, if the question is not relevant to the study, then leave it out.

Respondents give up their own time to answer surveys and irrelevant questions are likely to irritate them.

2 Language

Think carefully about the language you are using and keep it clear and simple. Choose words that are straightforward and that people will understand.

3 Open questions vs closed questions

Closed questions are more common in surveys, but are more limiting in the responses they generate. They generally have a Yes or No answer, or there are a number of predetermined responses for the respondent to choose from.

Example of closed question

How often do you come to this day centre?

Every day ☐

4–6 days per week ☐

2–3 days per week ☐

1 day per week ☐

This type of question is useful, as surveys often cover facts. With surveys, it is also reasonable to guess the range of possible responses. They are also easier for the researcher to complete as they often involve them only in ticking a box rather than writing freehand.

Remember when classifying age groups, that there shouldn't be any cross-over in the age spans. Groups should be classified into clear age groups, e.g. under 18, 18–34, 35–49, 50–64, and so on, and not 18, 18–35, 35–50, 50–65. This will ensure that those who are 18, 35 or 50 will know which category to tick.

Closed questions are far easier to analyse and results can be presented effectively as graphs and charts. Such graphical presentation can enhance the work and can clarify the findings for the reader.

If you are going to use pre-selected responses, it is important that you think about these to ensure that they have clear meanings and that they are sufficiently different for the respondent to be able to make a definite choice.

Example

How do you rate the day centre's facilities?

Poor ☐

Average ☐

Good ☐

Each respondent will have a different measurement of poor, average and good. It is difficult to make comparisons as one person's 'good' will be another person's 'average'. The statements are not quantifiable enough.

Other words which lack clear meaning include 'reasonable' and 'adequate'.

Open questions are those which allow free response by the respondent.

Such questions generate a wide range of responses and can make analysis more difficult. However, they do give a more personal insight into the respondents' thoughts. This type of question is useful if you are unsure about the range of possible responses you may get.

Example:

Why do you use the day centre?

4 Personal information

Respondents are more likely to answer questions on personal information, such as age or income, if the answer required is within a range rather than specific. Therefore, closed questions are best for this type of question.

EXAMPLE

Is your age group

<20 [ ]   20–30 [ ]   31–40 [ ]   41–50 [ ]

(**Note**: the symbol < means under or below)

Remember, people do not like giving out personal information, so ask only if it is absolutely relevant and necessary for the research. This should also be obvious to the respondents.

If you do need to ask for personal information, it is often suggested that the questions should be put at the end of the survey. Personal questions at the start may put people off doing the survey for you. They might just walk away.

5 Multiple questions

Make sure questions ask respondents for only one answer. Avoid asking a question which is really more than one question.

Breaking up a question into separate parts will ensure that all respondents are clearly directed into answering all questions.

6 Assumptions

Try to avoid questions that presume something about the opinions or actions of the respondent. This also applies to knowledge and experiences. For example, if you put the question 'Do you like meals on wheels?' to all elderly people, it assumes they all have that service.

You need to be sure that every question asks something that the respondent can reasonably answer.

7 Leading questions

It is easy to devise questions which suggest a preferred response, particularly if the researcher feels a particular way.

ACTIVITY

Give an example of a leading question.

Leading questions can lead to bias in the answers you receive. Therefore, it is important that you check your questions rigorously before you carry out the survey.

Organising the survey

Make sure the questions are presented and asked in a logical order. Once you draft the questions, group them in an ordered way, so that, where appropriate, one question leads to another.

One way of doing this is to write the draft questions on small pieces of card or postcards. You can then order and reorder them until you are happy with the order, without having to rewrite the questions every time. Once you are happy with the order, the survey can be typed up and reproduced as many times as is necessary.

Piloting a data collection survey

Once you have completed the survey questions, test them out on a small number of people, or on a small scale if just recording information, to identify any areas you have missed. Always have an objective look at the work, and perhaps ask someone else to comment on it. Sometimes, when you have been working closely on something, it is difficult for you to see the errors, mistakes or confusing questions because you are so close to the work. To you it may be obvious what you mean when constructing the survey, but in practice this may not be the case.

This process is called a 'pilot'. Test the survey on five people or record five pieces of information. This should tell you whether the survey, as you have set it up, is going to work.

Data collection surveys which record information

A survey is also a way of recording information relevant to the topic but one which does not require input from individuals. For example, a researcher looking at how the elderly get to a day centre may choose to carry out a survey which involves recording how people arrive. They may not need to talk to anyone to collect this information, just stand outside the day centre and note down the mode of transport.

An example of a simple tally chart is given below.

EXAMPLE

Title: A survey of the way clients arrive at St John's Day Centre	
Day: Tuesday 19th February Time: 8.30–9.00 am	
Car	IIII
Bicycle	I
Taxi	III
Voluntary bus	IIII
Public transport	II

It is still important to think carefully about the categories which you are using as part of the survey and the detail that you want to collect.

It is possible to collect too few details, so that the survey does not really tell you anything of value; or to collect too much information, and so lose the focus of the survey. It is also important to think about the circumstances in which you are carrying out the survey. If you are recording information which is static, you will be able to note down more details than information about a moving source, e.g. a traffic survey.

A survey can therefore take either the form of a simple tally chart or something which contains more complicated questions.

Collating the results from a data collection survey

The results of the survey are best presented in a format which shows the overall responses, such as a tally chart or a results table. It is then worth presenting certain aspects of the survey in a graphical or pictorial format. The responses given to the questions will often determine which is the best type of graph or chart to use. You should choose a method which helps display the responses in a clear format. Charts and graphs help the reader understand the information more easily.

Conclusion

It is important that you also draw a conclusion from the survey. You should identify what you think your results show you in terms of the aim of the survey.

Evaluating a data collection survey

An evaluation should look at how effective the survey was in collecting the information it set out to get. If the survey is one which involves asking questions, you need to analyse how effective the questions were in gaining the information that was required. You may choose to ask yourself the following questions:

◆ Were the questions clear?

◆ Was the language understandable?

◆ Did the questions get the information that was required?

◆ Was the survey the right length?

◆ Was the survey carried out in the right place?

◆ Were there enough respondents to get a clear picture?

With a survey which does not involve asking people questions, you may need to ask yourself:

◆ Was the survey carried out over a long enough time span?

◆ Would the results be different if the survey was carried out at a different time of the week or in a different place?

◆ Was the information collected detailed enough?

◆ Did it cover all the necessary material?

ACTIVITY

Study the data collection survey below.

Survey on Year 1 children's sweet-eating habits

1   Do you have children?   Yes ☐   No ☐

2   How many?

3   Which age groups?   4–5 ☐   5–6 ☐   6–7 ☐

4   How many times per day do they eat sweets?

    0–1   ☐

    1–2   ☐

    2.5–3   ☐

    3–4   ☐

5   When do they tend to eat sweets?

    Before breakfast   ☐

    Lunchtime   ☐

    After school   ☐

    Throughout the day   ☐

6   What are their favourite sweets?

7   Who buys their sweets?

    You   ☐

    Other relatives   ☐

    They buy them themselves ☐

    Other   ☐

Thank you for your co-operation.

Questions

1   Does the survey make sense?

2   Are the questions appropriate?

3   Is there any other information that you feel this survey should have collected?

4   Where do you feel it could be carried out?

5   Is it the best primary research method in which to collect this type of information?

6   Would you feel happy carrying out this survey?

Further Reading

Bell, J (1999) *Doing your research project*, Open University Press, Buckingham

Green, S (2000) *Research methods*, Stanley Thornes, Cheltenham

4

Doing your research project

11 Planning and carrying out your research project

As the earlier chapters in this book have shown, research can be carried out in a variety of ways. It can be used to explore almost any topic and is a useful tool to help make predictions and estimates. Most advanced courses require students to develop research skills as part of their syllabus.

Research can be undertaken on a small or large scale. It can be used to support an argument in an essay or be a major piece of work. Many subjects require students to undertake a major investigation. This chapter will focus on how to plan and organise your research project successfully. The chapter will cover:

◆ Deciding on your area of study

◆ Ensuring the area of study is right

◆ Developing the title or hypothesis

◆ Double-checking the potential of the title or hypothesis

◆ Developing aims and objectives

◆ Effective planning

◆ Secondary research

◆ Effective time management

◆ Effective communication.

Good planning is the key to a successful investigation. Planning takes time and it may seem as if you are making very slow progress. However, systematic planning at the start can help ensure you do not start on an unachievable course and waste time later on.

TIP

Avoid rushing into your work. Take time to think your ideas through and plan. Planning any research project obviously starts with deciding on your area of study and from this your title or hypothesis.

Deciding on your area of study

All research projects begin with a decision on what to investigate. It is important that the area of study is focused enough to carry out an achievable piece of work. The breadth of the study will depend on the time over which it is to be carried out and the resources available to you.

Begin by identifying an area of study which interests you. At this stage, it could be a very broad topic area, such as abortion, or something more focused, such as the Literacy Hour in primary schools.

It is important to identify a focus to the work, which will suit your time scale and resources.

A title such as 'Single-parent Families' is too vague and wide for a study. You could write a book on this topic. For a research project you need to have a narrower, more clearly defined focus: for example, you may choose to focus on childcare options used by single-parent families or on attitudes to single-parent families.

In order to identify the best topic area and potential title, it is a good idea to identify several different options. Use the planning sheet below to help with this first stage of the process.

Research Planning Sheet

Possible areas/topics of interest

Potential titles

Final title

Signed Tutor............................. **Student**............................. **Date**............

Part of the planning process involves appreciating the types of resources that are available to you. Many research projects undertaken by students have both a time and resource limit; it is important, therefore, that the focus of the work is not unrealistic. It is generally not possible to carry out a piece of research which reflects the whole of the country. Some of the best research investigations focus on a locality or on a particular age group which is readily available for research purposes – for example, adolescents.

Compare the two titles below.

1 To what extent are adolescents health conscious?

or

To what extent are people health conscious?

2 To what extent do childcare facilities meet the needs of working parents?

or

To what extent do childcare facilities meet the needs of working parents in the X area of X?

Can you see the advantage of focusing on a particular area or age group? It immediately focuses the title and makes the work more manageable.

Ensuring the area of study is right

Once you have decided on the topic which you think has the most potential, you need to establish if it will offer the scope you need to develop a worthwhile investigation. This is best achieved by going through several planned stages.

First begin by brainstorming the topic area. This process is sometimes called a web diagram, spider diagram or a mind map. An example is given below.

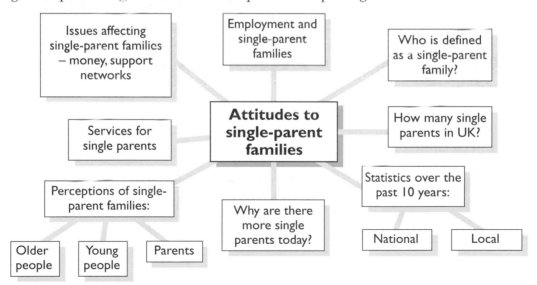

A mind map/spider diagram on attitudes to single-parent families

Basically, this involves noting down all the ideas you have that are linked to the area of study. You should write down everything that comes into your mind as you are doing this, as it will help you to see the full extent of the topic. New ideas may well come out of this process and it can help identify the breadth of the topic.

As you jot down the ideas, areas of thought can be extended to show how they might be developed, such as in the perceptions section in the diagram on page 171 which has been extended to show whose views could be investigated.

The diagram can be as complex as you wish. It can also be developed to include the investigatory methods that might be used to achieve each aspect of the diagram. Alternatively, this could be a separate web diagram. It is also useful to write an explanation of the diagram as this helps the examiner to see your full range of thinking.

Developing the title or hypothesis

At this point, provided the area of study looks promising, you should establish the title or hypothesis.

Formulating the title as a question can help to ensure you develop an investigative approach rather that a project approach. For example, the title 'Single-parent Families' can lend itself to a 'cut and stick' approach, whereas a title such as 'To what extent have attitudes to single-parent families changed?' will encourage more of a research approach. However, this title may suggest a previously poor attitude, which is something you may wish to avoid saying. The title could be developed into 'To what extent are single-parent families accepted as another family type in today's society?'

Avoid questions which have a Yes/No answer, as this can limit the scope of the work, e.g. 'Have attitudes to single-parent families changed?'

Another approach is to develop a hypothesis rather than a title. A hypothesis is a statement which the study aims to support, or not, according to the findings.

For example:

'Attitudes to single-parent families are poor. People think it is not a good family structure in which to bring up children'.

Double-checking the potential of the title or hypothesis

Having done the brainstorm and developed a title or hypothesis, you should double-check that the area of study has the potential you think it has. A double-checking process can be completed by doing a check on its potential for primary and secondary research.

To do this, you need to think about the different research methods which could be used and how you might apply them to the area of study. The grid opposite gives you a format for doing this.

Research methods check sheet			
PROPOSED TITLE:			
Research method	**To be used? Yes/No**	**Explanation of how the technique will be used**	**How will the results be recorded?**
Secondary research using textbooks			
Letters			
Visits			
Questionnaires			
Survey			
Interviews			
Video/film			
Newspapers/ magazines			
Experimental work			
Observations			
Consumer information analysis			
Internet			
Other methods			

Example of a used research methods check sheet:

Research methods check sheet			
PROPOSED TITLE: To what extent does the state pension cover the basic needs of the elderly?			
Research method	**To be used? Yes/No**	**Explanation of how the technique will be used**	**How will the results be recorded?**
Secondary research using text books	Yes	Research into state pensions and amounts Other research on elderly income	Written
Letters	Yes	Age Concern Benefits Agency	Written
Visits			
Questionnaires	Yes	To a number of elderly people to find out how they spend their pension	Graphs, charts
Survey			
Interviews	Yes	Elderly people for more in-depth information on spending	Tape
Video/film			
Newspapers/ magazines	Yes	Articles on elderly income and expenditure	Table/written
Experimental work			
Observations			
Consumer information analysis			
Internet	Yes	Research for up-to-date information Data from the Stationery Office	Written
Other methods			

You need now to consider the requirements of your research project against the potential of the study.

Some investigations must include primary research methods, such as questionnaires or interviews, which you must carry out yourself. Others allow you to do a piece of work which is entirely based on secondary sources, such as research from textbooks.

After completing the checklist, if your area of study lends itself only to secondary research but you need to include primary research methods, you will need to reconsider the potential of the study. It may be possible to develop the focus of the study to allow some primary research. If this isn't possible, it is best to abandon the study at this point and develop another topic area.

It is better to abandon the work at this early stage before carrying out in-depth research, only to have to change at a later point.

This shows why time spent planning is essential.

Developing aims and objectives

Aims and objectives help focus the work and clearly set out the boundaries within which the study will be carried out.

Aims

These are broad statements which identify what the study hopes to find out. They further clarify the title or hypothesis and outline the angle the study will take. For example:

♦ To establish the number of single-parent families in the UK today.

♦ To appreciate attitudes towards single parent families as a modern family unit.

♦ To explore the range of support services available to single-parent families.

Aims generally begin with verbs which describe what the work hopes to achieve through the research methods that are used. These commonly are.

- to explore …
- to identify …
- to appreciate …
- to establish …
- to find out …
- to research …
- to discuss …

Objectives

These identify exactly how you intend to achieve your aims, and usually mention a method of research. Here are some examples of objectives:

♦ To research statistics for single-parent families, using national statistics such as the Census, *Social Trends*, etc.

♦ To devise a questionnaire to establish individuals' views on single-parent families.

♦ To carry out interviews with single parents on their perceptions of attitudes towards them.

In total, the objectives should enable you to achieve all your aims. It may be that an aim can be achieved through two different objectives. For example, both questionnaires and interviews in the examples given would seek to achieve the second aim on attitudes towards single parents.

The work on the title, the web diagram, the methods checklist and the aims and objectives ensures a good foundation on which to develop the rest of the study.

Effective planning

The next step involves developing a good plan, which will help the study remain on track.

A good plan sets out what you intend to do and why. It also allows you to monitor your progress and allows changes to be made.

Plans are most useful if they are divided into sections using clearly defined headings. An example of a detailed action plan is given on pages 177–180. It is a plan for an investigation called:

'To what extent is bottled water becoming a popular drink for adolescents due to its healthy image?'

It is important that a plan is flexible. Research projects do not always go according to plan and you must be able to make changes to the plan to reflect this. Also, the primary research may throw up issues or areas of interest which you wish to develop further if they are relevant to the topic. This means that you will need to remain adaptable and amend your plan as necessary.

Secondary research

It is important you begin your work by reading around your subject area. This will inform you about the theories that already surround your topic. It will also give you an overview of what other research has been carried out in this area.

Carrying out the research methods

How to carry out the different research methods you have chosen has been covered in different chapters of the book, however there are two skills which will help you to do this effectively – effective time management and good communication skills.

Effective time management

Many research projects are poor because of poor time management. Students are well known for not managing their time well. In an extensive piece of work such as a research project, this can be fatal to the success of the work. Most research projects cannot be carried out solely by using secondary source material and tend to include some elements of primary research. The time taken to carry out the research should not be underestimated.

It is a common mistake to underestimate how long it takes to carry out research, as often studies have long deadlines and students focus on more immediate work. When the deadline approaches, students start work in earnest, only to realise that they do not have enough time to do a good piece of work. This will weaken the research and perhaps affect the final result.

Action Plan

What do I need to do?	How will I do it?	Why?	Materials needed?	Cost?	Achieved?	If not, next step?
Think about topics of interest and areas I might like to study for my investigation	Look at all possible areas to choose from and decide which area I would most like to study	So I can choose the best possible topic to suit my interests and begin to plan out a possible title for my investigation	–	–	Yes	–
Having chosen a topic, choose a possible title for my investigation	Make several titles up from my topic area and then choose the most suitable one	So I can choose from a list of titles my favourite one to study	–	–	Yes	–
Make a list of aims and objectives for the investigation	Through planning out the methods I am going to use to research my topic and through deciding what I need to achieve to complete this investigation	So I can have a set of aims and objectives to follow through whilst working on the assignment, and so I know all along what I am trying to achieve	Written title for the investigation	–	Yes	–
Draw a spider diagram with explanations	By writing the title in the middle of the page and then by writing everything I am going to do for this investigation through planning, research and implementation	So I have a diagram to follow while working on this assignment that explains everything I have to do and why I have to do it	Title for investigation Aims and objectives of the assignment	–	Yes	–

What do I need to do?	How will I do it?	Why?	Materials needed?	Cost?	Achieved?	If not, next step?
Write a statement showing why I have chosen this particular topic and title	By writing down exactly why I chose this topic and the title I did, stating my reasons for choice	So I can put it into my report on the investigation and so I can show what interests me most about the topic and title I have chosen	–	–	Yes	–
Carry out some research into the consumption of bottled water, looking at the main sources, how it is bottled, how healthy it is and its popularity within the population	By looking in the college library and the relevant department at college for books giving me information in this area and highlighting the important parts	So that I know some facts about bottled water before I go any further into my investigation	Books and *Which?* magazines from the library	–	Yes	–
Write letters to send out to different bottled water companies	By writing a letter to them asking for all the relevant information I need to investigate further	So I can find out the companies' sales figures for the last five years, any information on mineral content, production methods including testing, and any publicity material so I can draw conclusions from the results	Letter-headed paper from college	12 × 26p = £3.12	Yes	–
Watch a video on the health aspects of bottled water and where it comes from	Watch the video and make relevant notes while it is playing	So I can bring together all of my results and draw conclusions from it	The video	–	Yes	–

				Cost	Maths	
Put together a survey for me to carry out in various shops	By deciding on a suitable sample, deciding on what information I need and then visiting the outlets to gain the information	So I can take a look at the different brands, shelf space given, prices per litre and sizes available in all the different types of shops	Drawn survey chart	–	Yes	–
Put together a questionnaire to give to twenty adolescents to fill in and then return to me	Write a series of questions to put to the people to find out about their drinking habits of bottled water, and what preferences they have if any	So I can find out exactly how popular bottled water is amongst people of this age range	Questionnaire	–	Yes	–
Devise a Taste Test to put to ten participants at college	Think of a series of tests which I could use to find out people's preferences and to see if they can tell the difference between different types of bottled water	So I can collate my results and draw conclusions about the popularity of bottled water	Samples of water and prepared test answer sheets	4×36 $= 1.44$ $+$ 2×34 $= 68p$ $= £2.12$	Yes	–
Having completed all of my methods of research, complete a write-up of each one	By writing my aims, methods and conclusions drawn for each method of research and, in some cases, drawing appropriate bar graphs and charts to illustrate results	So I can clearly see how I went about each method and the results I got from it, including any conclusions I have drawn	All of the relevant materials from the methods of research	–	Yes	–

What do I need to do?	How will I do it?	Why?	Materials needed?	Cost?	Achieved?	If not, next step?
Write my report	Through writing my reasons for choosing this particular topic area, my aims and objectives; through using every research method I carried out to explain results and conclusions I reached; and also writing an evaluation of each method I used, and the whole investigation in general	So I can give a clear report on the results I have found and the conclusions I have drawn. Also so I can critically evaluate all of my work for this investigation, stating any future developments and ways in which I would change or improve what I have done for this investigation	Aims and objectives, statement of why I have chosen this topic, and every write-up of all the research methods I used for this investigation	–	Yes	–
A front cover for the assignment	Through using the scanner at college and Microsoft PowerPoint on the computer, I will design my own front cover	So I can have a front cover which gives the title of my investigation	The scanner at college and Microsoft PowerPoint computer program	–	Yes	–

Tips for effective time management

◆ Start straight away – do not put it off.

◆ Carry out work on the study at regular intervals.

◆ Develop a time plan and stick to it.

◆ Follow your main plan and monitor your progress – if you fall behind, allocate some more time the following week to ensure you remain on track.

◆ Plan regular review sessions with your tutor – this will give you a target to aim for. Set yourself goals which you want to achieve by each of these sessions.

Effective communication

An effective research process relies heavily on good communication skills. These are skills in speaking, listening and writing. Communication which uses words is known as verbal communication skills. However, a lot of communication takes place without anything being said, for example through the look on someone's face or the body language they are using. This is known as non-verbal communication.

Whatever research methods you choose to use, even if your work is based 100% on secondary sources, you will draw on aspects of these skills. The more you use primary research, the more verbal and non-verbal communication skills will be used.

Non-verbal communication skills

Non-verbal communication covers a wide range of actions.

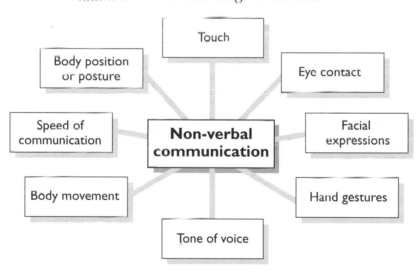

There are various ways we communicate non-verbally

Non-verbal communication sends messages to people without having to use words. It can help a conversation move forward, but the wrong body language or facial expression can stop someone talking to you and therefore making the communication ineffective.

ACTIVITY

Think about the different research methods.
List the communication skills you think are needed for each.
Place them in order, in terms of the most important for that method first.

I   Are there any which do not draw on communication skills at all?

2   Is there any skill which is used more than any other? Why do you think this is?

Communicating effectively in the research process

When you are carrying out research, the most important task is to make sure you get all the information you need. To do this, you need to draw on all the communication skills you have. You will need to make the most of both verbal and non-verbal communication skills.

Effective listening

Listening will be used in research methods such as interviews and observations. Listening means hearing what someone is saying, thinking about it and trying to understand what he or she means. It will also draw on your ability to remember, especially if the respondent talks for a long time. It also involves planning what you are going to say back to them. Listening well and responding to what has been said is hard work as it needs a lot of concentration.

Reflective listening

Reflective listening means listening hard to what other people are saying, and reflecting back their views and ideas in what you say, to make sure you have understood them correctly. For example:

Person 1   'If women work full time when children are young, this can have a detrimental effect on the development of the child.'

Person 2   'So you think that women should stay at home?'

Person 2 is reflecting back what Person 1 has said in a shortened format. This allows him to check if he has understood what the other person is saying and also encourages the other person to keep talking.

In the research situation, you want the person you are talking to to give you as much information as she can. There are a number of ways to help this to happen:

◆ Use positive non-verbal communication – nodding, good eye contact and smiling can encourage someone to keep talking.

◆ Think about the position you are sitting in and the atmosphere of the room – a comfortable room, not too hot or cold, with comfortable chairs will help the communication process.

◆ Use reflective listening skills – recap what the person has said to you to show you are listening. This will encourage them to continue.

Can you think of a situation where you were talking to someone but you didn't think he or she was listening?

What made you think you didn't have his or her full attention?

How did this make you feel?

What effect did it have on the conversation?

Many people think they are listening, when actually their mind is drifting off on to other topics, which means they are not fully taking in what is being said. In effect, they are not listening. Often, the person speaking picks this up. Although the person they are talking to may be nodding as if he is listening, he may be looking around the room rather than making eye contact, or he may be drumming his fingers on the table, or simply not be responding as expected. There are many other 'clues' that people give that they are not really listening, including body movements or facial expressions.

Research methods such as interviews rely on you being able to get as much information from the respondent as possible. Therefore, you need to make sure you listen in order to do this.

ACTIVITY

1 Explain why planning is important.

2 Give three examples of non-verbal communication.

3 What is reflective listening?

4 What is the difference between aims and objectives?

5 What is a hypothesis?

6 What sections should be on a planning table?

7 Why is it important to manage your time effectively when carrying out your research project?

Further reading

Bell, J (1999) *Doing your research project*, Open University Press, Buckingham
Green, S (2000) *Research methods*, Stanley Thornes, Cheltenham

12 Presenting your work

In most situations, you will write up the bulk of your research work as you go along. However, you will need to pull it all together at the end. This may be through a report or a discussion of the findings. In this section, you will make links between the findings from the different research methods you have used. The aim will be to identify, for the reader, the conclusions you have drawn as a result of your work.

Good presentation at this stage is essential. Research projects can be difficult for the unfamiliar reader to get around. They just want to read or hear the salient points. A disorganised presentation will put a reader off. Having put a lot of effort into the process, it is worth presenting it in an organised fashion in order to get maximum marks.

This chapter looks at how to present your work in the most effective manner. It covers

◆ Writing up your main findings

◆ Structuring a research write-up

◆ Writing up the appendices

◆ Presenting your research methods

◆ Evaluation as part of the appendices.

Writing up your main findings

Generally, research projects are written up in well-defined sections. As with most pieces of work, they have a beginning, a middle and an end. The middle is generally sub-sectioned. It can reflect a sandwich with the bread being the beginning and the end, and the middle being the different layers of filling.

There is no right or wrong way of writing up a research project. However, work that is done for an examination has to meet certain criteria. You need to make sure you know what is required if your work is for an external examination.

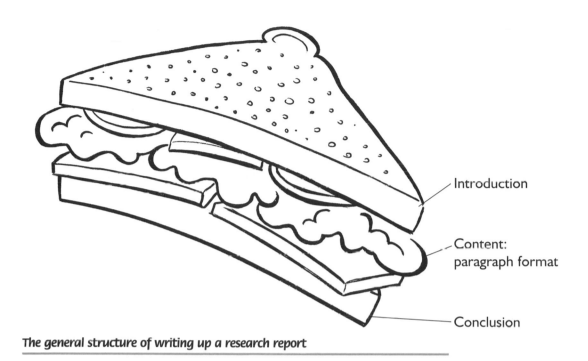

Introduction

Content: paragraph format

Conclusion

The general structure of writing up a research report

Structuring a research write-up

The following is a set of headings that can be used for structuring a research project write-up

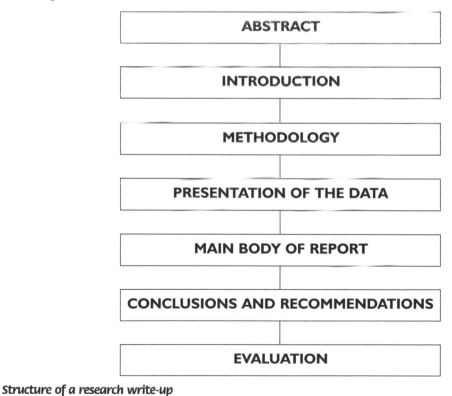

ABSTRACT

INTRODUCTION

METHODOLOGY

PRESENTATION OF THE DATA

MAIN BODY OF REPORT

CONCLUSIONS AND RECOMMENDATIONS

EVALUATION

Structure of a research write-up

Abstract

This is a brief summary of what the project is about and the general approach. An abstract is very brief, usually no longer than half a page. It is similar to the brief overview you find on the back of novels.

This piece of research involved a detailed look at the MMR vaccination and its links with autism. The work begins with a summary of the research around the topic of vaccinations, the MMR and the suggested links with autism. It then outlines the methodology which is being used to explore the issues. The findings of the primary research are then related to the literature review.

The work explores the concerns the general public has about the potential effects of the MMR on children. It also compares these views with the medical view. In doing this, it tries to present a balanced discussion of the arguments.

Finally, the work is drawn to a conclusion and tries to establish the facts.

Introduction

This is a detailed outline of the aims and objectives of the work. It is often written as a rough draft at the start of the project as it helps give direction to the work. It is then finalised at a later date to ensure it covers exactly what happened, and to allow for changes as the research process takes place. If you are using a hypothesis, this will also be in part of this section.

Methodology

This is a discussion of the method you have chosen to use in your project. You should explain how your research methods divide between secondary and primary methods. You need to identify the qualitative and quantitative methods you have used and outline why you have chosen these particular methods. You should also explain the choice of sampling methods you have used. Include discussion of all the considerations you have made, including ethnic and cultural issues, and the confidentiality principle, including the Data Protection Act. You should also discuss how ethics have affected the methods you have used.

You should discuss the factors which may affect the validity and reliability of the data collected, such as:

◆ Respondents not being open or not giving a true picture.

◆ Factors which may have influenced the data collection, such as the environment in which data collection took place, e.g.

- If in a group setting, could this have affected what an individual said; did it allow all individuals to participate equally; did anyone dominate?
- If carrying out a survey on the street, were people able to give adequate and considered responses or were they in a rush to go somewhere?

Any factor which could have influenced the results should be mentioned as this shows the reader that you are aware of the restraints on your work.

Presentation of the data

In this section, you need to give a statistical representation of the results you gained through the various methods of research. These should be labelled correctly and presented in the order that they are discussed in the main body of the text.

Main body

This is where the major discussion of the findings takes place. There should be clear reference to the data section. You may choose to note the problems that arose in this section as you address the findings.

Conclusion and recommendations

This is where you need to draw together the overall findings from the work and make your conclusions and recommendations.

Evaluation

This is the section where you need to reflect on the work that has been done and assess its strengths and weaknesses. In all cases, evaluative comments must assess how it affected the work. The most successful way to do this is to approach it in a systematic way. It may help you to do this if you use a series of questions.

Planning

Begin by evaluating your approach to planning the work and how successful it was.

- Did you plan it well?
- Did you have an effective written plan?
- Did you keep to your plan? If so, how did that help you achieve the completed project?
- If not, how did that affect the progress of the work? Why didn't the plan work? What could you have done differently to make it more successful?
- How would you change your planning if you were doing this again, and why?

Secondary research

Think about the different sources of secondary research used and assess how they contributed to the success of the work

- Did you use an effective range of secondary research?
- Did you use search methods effectively? How did they help the process of gathering secondary material?
- Were the sources used up to date?
- Were the sources used valid and reliable?
- Did you feel you carried out enough secondary research before you started the primary research?

◆ How did the results from the secondary research help you with your primary research?

◆ Would you have used any additional secondary sources? If so, why; if not, why not?

◆ Did you record the information from your secondary research effectively?

◆ How did you use this as you progressed through the project?

◆ Did you use your time effectively while doing the secondary research?

Primary research methods

You should evaluate **each** primary method used separately. This will ensure that you cover each one in adequate depth. The following trigger questions can be applied to most primary research methods.

◆ Was this an effective choice of research method for the topic chosen?

◆ Did you plan the method well?

◆ Was the sample used appropriate?

◆ Did the method gain the information that you hoped for? How did that help the work?

◆ If the method wasn't successful in gaining the appropriate information, why was that? How did that affect the work?

◆ How might you change the method if you were doing it again? Why would you do this? How would it improve the work?

◆ Were the results presented appropriately?

To draw the evaluation together, you may also identify overall strengths and weaknesses in the work. You need to be able to justify why you feel something was a strength or weakness.

Future developments

You may be asked to highlight how you might progress with the work if you were to continue with it from the point at which you stopped. Any suggestions should be relevant to the work carried out so far and be realistic. It may be necessary to give a brief outline of what you would do.

Bibliography

This is a list of all the sources used for information. You should list any texts which you have looked at – the extent to which they have been used is not important. If you have looked at a text for ideas or to read something relevant to the work, it must be listed. The bibliography should be written using the Harvard method which is explained in Chapter 3.

Appendices

This section contains any relevant information which is referred to in the write-up but doesn't fit into any of the sections themselves. It is important that the information included is relevant and illuminates the work in some way. It should not be used as a way to bulk up the project. If it's not relevant, don't put it in.

Appendices should be relevant to the research project and not used as a way of bulking it up

Other ways of writing up research

Another approach is needed if an overall report of a particular length is required, for example 2,000–3,000 words. In this case, the same information is required but it may be presented in a different way. The sections might be divided into the report, and appendices which contain all the supplementary information.

Using this approach, the report would be constructed as follows:

Analysis

An outline of what the work is about and why it has been chosen.

Aims and objectives

◆ The aims of the work – states what you hope to achieve by the end of the project.

◆ The objectives of the work set out how you intend to achieve the aims. Objectives generally include reference to a research method.

EXAMPLE

Aim:	To establish young people's thoughts and beliefs about the effects of smoking on the body.
Objective:	To use a questionnaire to establish young people's knowledge of smoking and its effects on health.

Try it out

Identify which of the following statements is an aim or an objective.

1 To identify the incidence of drinking amongst 14- to 16-year-olds.

2 To carry out an interview with day-care clients to establish how far the service meets their needs.

3 To explore the range of benefits available to single-parent families.

4 To appreciate the nutritional needs of a person with coeliac disease.

5 To devise and carry out a survey of the range of diabetic foods available on the market.

6 To research into genetically modified foods using the Internet, textbooks and magazines.

Answers
1, 3 and 4 are aims
2, 5 and 6 are objectives

The section on page 191 gives an example of aims and objectives from a report. The investigation was entitled 'To what extent are adolescents aware of their dietary requirements?'

Documentation

As you write the main section of the report, it is important that you mention each method that you have used and refer to the detail in the appendices. The reader will then be able to look at your methods and findings in detail. When the word count is small, it is important that you use the appendices as effectively as possible to support the report.

The table on pages 193–195 explains how the appendices should be laid out.

Implementation

This section should broadly be a discussion of the conclusions drawn as a result of the different research methods. The conclusions should be supported with discussion of the findings, using facts and figures acquired as evidence to support the points made. It should not be a section where you just list the results gained. The skill is in being able to interpret the results into some meaningful conclusions and decisions.

Example of aims and objectives

Aims

◆ To investigate the recommended dietary requirements for adolescents.

◆ To establish sources from which adolescents gain their dietary advice.

◆ To establish and assess the eating habits of the majority of adolescents.

◆ To establish adolescent preferences for 'healthy' foods.

◆ To outline the knowledge held by the majority of adolescents on diet and its relationship to health.

◆ To highlight the reasons behind the adolescents' consumption of a particular form of diet.

Objectives

◆ To investigate recommended dietary requirements through the researching of medical/biological texts, magazines, government reports (e.g. *Health of the Nation*) and the Internet.

◆ To interview adolescents to establish where they get most of their dietary advice.

◆ To devise and use questionnaires to find out the extent of adolescents' dietary knowledge.

◆ To conduct surveys and observations to assess the eating habits of adolescents in the college canteen.

◆ To carry out nutritional analysis of a number of diets to assess nutritional intake.

To show that you have really appreciated the inter-relationships of the research, you should try to link the findings of one research method to those of another. For example, a finding from a questionnaire may well support information found through secondary research.

This is generally the most difficult section of any research as it draws on higher-level skills of being able to look beyond the results gained to see patterns and trends emerging.

An extract from the implementation section of a report is given below. The conclusions are <u>underlined</u>. You can see how the student has successfully drawn conclusions and supports them with results from the research. You will also note that the student refers to the appendices at various points in the report. This ensures that the reader looks at the detail of the research methods undertaken as well as at the overall findings.

Extract from a report 'To what extent are adolescents aware of their dietary requirements?'

In order to assist in establishing conclusions from the interview, a dietary analysis (Appendix 6) of the weekly diet was conducted and dietary tables completed. This revealed that in their 'typical diet' adolescents failed to consume some essential nutrients and other essential vitamins and minerals in the correct recommended amounts. For example, protein content appeared to be either considerably over or under the recommended amounts for both male and female adolescents. Furthermore, the majority of protein was derived from foods with a high saturated fat content. In turn, such foods contributed to the extremely high levels of fat which formed part of the diet. Fat intake far exceeded the 30% of total energy intake as recommended by health experts.

   The interviews (Appendix 5) also influenced me to the conclusion that the more unhealthy foods tend to be consumed during the middle of the day and not when adolescents are at home. In an attempt to add some substance to this conclusion, it appeared appropriate to conduct a survey for one week of foods purchased at lunchtimes (Appendix 7). The results obtained did support the previous conclusions. In addition, they led me to conclude that when adolescents are away from home, the food they choose is in accordance with their own tastes and this does not comply with dietary guidelines. It was also evident that the cheapest and largest majority of foods available in the canteen were high in fat and high in sugar but not particularly rich in essential vitamins and minerals. They therefore are not particularly suitable for an adolescent diet.

Evaluation

You must evaluate your work to show you appreciate the factors that have affected the effectiveness of the project. You need to evaluate each section of the work. This includes the planning and each research method, both primary and secondary, that you have undertaken. Follow the guidelines given in the section on evaluation on page 187. This will ensure that you complete the work in enough depth.

   An extract from an evaluation is given below. You can see that it is important that you relate any evaluative comments made to the effect they had on the success of the work.

Extract from an evaluation

Secondary research proved to be a particularly important part of the investigation as it gave me the background on which to build the rest of the research methods. The sources used were up to date and were easy to access. I also used the Internet, which proved to be a useful source of information.

   The use of questionnaires proved to be a worthwhile method of research. It enabled me to gather valuable information, which greatly influenced the direction of the rest of the investigation. The questionnaires were particularly effective due to their versatility. They allowed me to structure questions in order to gain a specific result which gave me a manageable amount of data to analyse.

Extract from an evaluation (continued)

The questionnaires were also effective in relation to time and money. This was also true for the interviews. Having identified my sample from the questionnaires, only a limited amount of time was needed for the interviews. However, the full results from the interviews did take longer than anticipated. This was due to the diaries I asked the subjects to keep for a week. I had to wait for their return and therefore the overall results of the interview could not be concluded until I had received them. This slowed my progress and it would have been better to have carried out the diary as a separate piece of research.

Writing up the appendices

Using this style of presentation, it is essential that each aspect of the work has an appendix related to it. The appendices are placed in a section at the end of the report. They should contain relevant information linked to the project which will serve to illuminate the report. It is, therefore, not useful to put in reams of notes copied from textbooks in the research section. It is more appropriate to put in brief, relevant notes if necessary. It is more important to provide a bibliography of any texts you have read which you have used to support your work.

The detail in this type of presentation about the method used is in the appendices. Therefore, these sections should be as comprehensive as possible. They contain all the evidence of the methods you have used in your research.

The appendices should be set out in an organised manner giving details of the work carried out. The appendix should be divided into sections and labelled with a letter or a number. In general, each section will represent a method. It doesn't particularly matter which appendix comes first but generally it is helpful to present them in the order that you used the research methods. The chart below sets out suggestions for the contents of each appendix as relevant to that method.

Presenting your research methods

Suggestions for contents of appendices

1   Research
- Magazine articles/photocopies of pages from a book – highlighted
- Extracts from a book in note form
- CD-ROM printout – highlighted
- Bibliography of books read/used to support the work, and written up using the Harvard method

In all cases, there should be a note of the source on the extract/notes.

2   Planning section
- Planning table
- Action plan giving time scales
- Spider diagram/initial notes to show the thinking in the design of the work

3 Letters

◆ Aim

◆ Copy of the letter sent

◆ List of addresses the letter was sent to

◆ Any replies

◆ Relevant material from replies

◆ Written summary from each reply

◆ Conclusions drawn from replies

4 Questionnaires

◆ Aim

◆ Method used to carry out the questionnaire, including the choice of sampling method

◆ Clean copy of the questionnaire

◆ Used copy of the questionnaire

◆ Summary of the results obtained

◆ Representation of the results as bar charts, pictograms, histograms, pie charts, etc. – this must be on graph paper/plain paper, not on lined paper. These diagrams should be labelled appropriately.

◆ Conclusions drawn from the results

5 Taste tests

◆ Aim

◆ Methods used, including the type of taste tests, with samples of the labels and a copy of the written instructions

◆ Copy of a used response sheet

◆ Collation of the results

◆ Representation of the results as for the questionnaire, as appropriate

◆ Conclusions

6 Interviews

◆ Aim

◆ Method, including how you chose your interviewees

◆ List of questions used if structured interview, or trigger questions planned if unstructured interview

◆ Results – as a taped or a written account

◆ Conclusions

7   Survey

- Aim
- Method used
- Completed survey
- Conclusions

8   Experimental work

- Aim
- Equipment/ingredients
- Method, including the variables and constants
- Results
- Conclusion

9   Consumer information analysis

- Aim
- Method chosen for analysis, including explanation of why these categories were chosen
- Examples of the materials used
- Results
- Conclusion

10   Newspaper articles/magazine analysis

- Aim
- Method, including range of papers used/reasons/time span of collection
- Articles (including source and date) – highlighted
- Conclusions

11   Videos

- Aim, with title and source (date if possible)
- Write-up of the main points of the video
- Conclusions drawn

In practice, each appendix should be written up as the research is carried out. Drawing conclusions for each section as you go along will ensure that the conclusions are drawn when the findings are fresh in your mind. Also, drawing conclusions at this stage will make the writing of the report far easier as you will have a wealth of material to draw on.

Generally, it is not necessary to evaluate each method used as part of the appendices as this forms part of the report. However, it will help you to write that section of the report if you make some notes as you go along.

Evaluation as part of the appendices

Some investigations suggest an appendix which draws together an evaluation of the entire work. This would follow the guidelines given earlier in the chapter.

If you are required to give future developments, it is often suggested that you give the detail of these as an appendix because of the word restrictions placed on the report.

If you are required to do this, you need to outline how you would approach achieving the future developments you have identified, and show how they could be a realistic extension of the work you have completed as part of your research. Students are often asked to do this, as it is recognised that a student investigation has limited time and resources attached to it and, therefore, it is not likely to be either original or complete.

An example of a good future development section is given below. It is based on future developments for an investigation into childcare facilities in one area of a local town.

> If I were to continue this piece of research I would aim to collect data from a broader field and compare the provision across areas of the town. It would be interesting to compare household statistics with provision, and see if there is any correlation between these.
> I would also like to interview local employers to find out if they feel there is adequate childcare provision to allow them to recruit and keep an appropriate workforce. It would also be interesting to investigate their perspective on the provision of subsidised childcare.

ACTIVITY

Think of an activity or exercise which you have recently carried out. This could be a piece of coursework for another subject, an activity which you have carried out on placement or an activity which you have planned and carried out as part of your social life.

Critically evaluate the success of that activity or exercise. Try to identify what went well and why, as well as what didn't work and why. Make sure you assess how the action taken affected the outcome.

Further reading

Bell, J (1999) *Doing your research project*, Open University Press, Buckingham
Green, S (2000) *Research methods*, Stanley Thornes, Cheltenham

Appendix I Useful addresses

Age Concern
Astral House
1268 London Road
London
SW16 4EJ

Alcohol Concern
305 Gray's Inn Road
London
WC1X 8QF

ASH (Action on Smoking and
Health)
Gloucester Place
London
EC1M 6BP

Association for Residential Care
The Old Rectory
Old Whittington
Chesterfield
Derbyshire
S41 9QY

British Institute of Mental
Handicap
Wolverhampton Road
Kidderminster
Worcestershire
DY10 3PP

Cancer Relief Macmillian Fund
Anchor House
15–19 Britten Street
London
SW3 3TZ

Centre for Policy on Ageing
25–31 Ironmonger Row
London
EC1V 3QP

Disabled Living Foundation
380–384 Harrow Road
London
W9 2HU

Family Policies Study Centre
231 Baker Street
London
NW1 6XE

Help the Aged
207–221 Pentonville Road
London
N1 9UZ

Institute of Race Relations
2–6 Leeke Street
King's Cross Road
London
WC1 9HS

Institute for the Study of Drug
Dependence
Waterbridge House
32–36 Loman Street
London
SE1 0EE

MACRE (Mental Aftercare
Association)
25 Bedford Square
London
WC1B 3HW

National Association of
Citizens' Advice Bureaux
Myddleton House
115–123 Pentonville Road
London
N1 9LZ

National Association of Councils
for Voluntary Service
3rd Floor
Arundel Court
177 Arundel Street
Sheffield
S1 2NU

National Childbirth Trust
Alexandra House
Oldham Terrace
Acton
London
W3 6NH

National Children's Bureau
8 Wakley Street
London
EC1V 7QE

National Council for One Parent
Families
225 Kentish Town Road
London
NW5 2LX

NSPCC (National Society for the
Prevention of Cruelty to
Children)
42 Curtain Road
London
EC2A 3NH

PHAB (Physically Disabled and
Able Bodied)
Summit House
Wandle Road
Croydon
Surrey
CR10 1DF

Pre School Learning Alliance
61–63 King's Cross Road
London
WC1W 9LL

RNIB (Royal National Institute
for the Blind)
224 Great Portland Street
London
W1N 6AA

Royal National Association for
the Deaf
105 Gower Street
London
WC1E 6AH

Royal Society of Health
RSH House
38a St George's Drive
London
SW1V 4BH

SHAC (The London Housing
Aid Centre)
189a Old Brompton Road
London
SW5 0AR

Terrence Higgins Trust
52–54 Gray's Inn Road
London
WC1X 8JU

Women's Health
52 Featherstone Street
London
EC1Y 9RT

Appendix 2 Links with Key Skills

What are Key Skills?

There are six key skills but three are called the 'First Key Skills'. These are:

◆ Communication

◆ Application of Number

◆ Information Technology.

The key skills cover the essential skills in each area which are needed by everyone whatever line of work they are in. Key skills are important as they:

◆ Assess the important skills that employers feel are important.

◆ Provide UCAS points for those who want to go on to higher education.

Key skills can be achieved at Level 1, 2 or 3. You can achieve each key skill at a different level.

Most advanced students will be aiming for Level 2 or Level 3 or a mixture of these across the key skills. Achieving all three key skill areas at Level 3 gives 60 UCAS points (20 per key skill). Level 2 key skills are awarded at 10 UCAS points each. Therefore, someone who achieved Level 3 communication and Level 2 application of number and IT would achieve 40 UCAS points.

To gain a key skill, you have to pass two aspects for each:

1 A test – this may be multiple-choice or open-ended questions, depending on the key skill and level. Level 3 IT is taken on a computer.

2 A portfolio – this is a file of work where you show that you can incorporate the key skills into your work.

The research aspect of health, social care and early years gives an ideal opportunity for you to produce evidence for the portfolio.

The table below shows how and where you can find the opportunities for key skills coverage at Level 3 in a research project. You need to approach your work carefully if you want to make sure you cover the key skills successfully.

Key skill	Requirement	Evidence produced in research project	Notes/special points
Communication			
C3.1a	Contribute to a discussion on a complex topic.	Involve the group in a discussion about the findings of your research project after the presentation for 3.1b.	Good way to produce effective evidence. Make sure someone completes a sheet about your contribution to the discussion as evidence.
C3.1b	Give a presentation.	Produce a presentation at the end of the research project for your peers on your work and your findings. If you use PowerPoint to produce your slides, this will also contribute to IT key skills.	Make sure you keep any notes and OHTs you use as evidence of what you did. You will also need to ask a teacher to assess the quality of your presentation using the assessment sheet.

Key skill	Requirement	Evidence produced in research project	Notes/special points
C3.2	Read and summarise information from documents (one must be an extended document of at least three pages).	You will do some secondary research as part of your project. You may use textbooks, newspaper articles or magazines. You should make sure you summarise two of the documents used as part of the secondary research section.	Make sure you keep copies of the original source material that you used to summarise from as part of the evidence for your key skills portfolio.
C3.3	Present an extended document on a complex topic. The text must be legible, with correct grammar, punctuation and spelling. It must also include one image.	Your report section of the research project is an extended document of at least three pages. You need to make sure that you include a diagram or image at an appropriate point in the text.	Make sure you check this carefully for spelling, punctuation and grammar as it is important that these are accurate for this key skill. If you are using IT to write the work up, make sure you use the spellchecker.
Application of Number			
AoN3.1	Plan and obtain numerical information. This should be from at least two sources.	You should always do a plan as part of your research project and this should show what data collection methods you intend to use and why. You should also explain your methods for data collection either in the report or in the appendices. You should be using more than two research methods as part of your work and therefore should be collecting data from at least two sources.	Remember that if you are aiming for Level 3, you need to collect at least 50 items of data for one data collection method. If aiming for Level 2, you need 20 items of data. Remember, to achieve Level 3 AoN, you must cover AoN3.1, 3.2 and 3.3 using the data collected.
AoN3.2	Carry out multi-stage calculations. These should include: ◆ Amounts and sizes ◆ Scales and proportions ◆ Statistics ◆ Rearranging and using formulae.	Analysis of findings of primary research, especially quantitative data such as that collected from questionnaires, will produce good opportunities to carry out multi-stage calculations. You will need to structure the questions carefully to make sure you have the opportunity to work with amounts, sizes, scales and proportions. Statistics and using formulae should occur fairly naturally as a result of calculations with the data collected.	As part of the piloting process of questionnaires and other primary research methods, check to make sure you will have the opportunity to carry out calculations across the four areas. Make sure you show all your workings for this aspect of the work.
AoN3.3	Present your findings using at least one graph, one chart and one diagram. Use the results of your calculations to support the views you present in your work.	Present the data collected in a range of appropriate formats including graphs, charts and diagrams. Make sure you refer to these in the write-up. In your appendices, justify why you have chosen the various methods of presentation rather than others.	Make sure you label your graphs, diagrams and charts correctly. Make sure you show a range of charts and graphs in your work.

Key skill	Requirement	Evidence produced in research project	Notes/special points
Information Technology			
IT3.1	Plan to collect information using IT.	As part of the secondary research section, you should use the Internet to complete a search on your chosen topic. You can also use CD-ROMs to search for information. This task should be listed as part of the plan that you produce at the start of the project. You must justify what material you have chosen to use, and what has been discarded and why, as part of the appendices.	Make sure you keep a record of the sites visited and any printouts you make.
IT3.2	Explore and develop information. Create new structures and information from the information.	You can use a spreadsheet package such as Excel to input and manipulate your data. This will allow you to produce graphs and charts from the data you have collected. You can then change and adapt the information to suit different purposes. You should be able to import charts and diagrams from the Excel package into a word document such as the report of the research. This will demonstrate how you have developed information.	Make sure you save the work on disk so you can put this in as evidence to support your work.
IT3.3	Present information, using IT.	Using packages such as Excel will allow you to show that you can present information using IT. You can also use Word to write up the report for the research project. Using IT in this way helps improve the presentation and makes it easier for the marker to read. It also allows you to make changes easily without having to rewrite the whole piece. The presentation for C3.1b could be produced on PowerPoint and this would allow you to show how you have developed information for a new purpose, i.e. from material for a research project to a presentation which will have a different target audience.	Keep any material you produce for the presentation as evidence.

In summary, if you apply opportunity for key skills evidence to the different stages of a research project, it looks like this:

Stage of the research project	Key skill signposting
Planning	AoN3.1 IT3.1
Secondary research	C3.2 IT3.1
Primary research methods – implementation	AoN3.1
Analysis of data, collation and presentation of results	AoN3.2 AoN3.3 IT3.2 IT3.3
Write-up of report	C3.3 IT3.2 IT3.3
Presentation based on the research project, using PowerPoint	C3.1b IT3.3
Discussion of the findings of the work following the presentation	C3.1b

It is possible to cover all the key skills through the research process, but this will depend on the topic which you have chosen to study. You need to be familiar with the key skills requirement from the outset and plan them into the work in the same way that you make sure that the work meets the criteria set for your main subject area. If you don't do this, then you will find that you have covered only part of the criteria and that further work will be needed to achieve the key skills.

Index